Home Education What? Why? How?

A Guide for Beginners

Sue Fairhead

Copyright © 2019 Sue Fairhead

All rights reserved. No part of this publication may be reproduced, distributed, or transmitted in any form or by any means, including photocopying, recording, or other electronic or mechanical methods, without the prior written permission of the publisher, except in the case of brief quotations embodied in critical reviews and certain other noncommercial uses permitted by copyright law. For permission requests, write to the author at the address below.

The right of Sue Fairhead to be identified as the Author of this Work has been asserted by her in accordance with the Copyright, Designs and Patents Act 1988.

Published by
Sue Fairhead
PO Box 42757
6503 Larnaca, Cyprus
Email: sueincyprus@home-ed.info

ISBN 978-1-79518-318-5

Cover design and book layout by Richard J Fairhead
Cover photo licensed from Storyblocks.com

Contents

Preface i
   Structure of the book v
   A note about pronouns vi

Part One

CHAPTER ONE: Why home educate? 1
   Legalities in brief 1
   Why home educate? 3
   Attitudes to schools 6
   Benefits of home education 9
CHAPTER TWO: How to home educate
(in theory) 13
   Parents as educators 13
   Is home education time-consuming? 17
   Motivation 23
CHAPTER THREE: How to home educate
(in practice) 31
   Getting Started 31
   Getting going 37
CHAPTER FOUR: What is education? 47
   What is education? 47
   Educational basics 54
   Learning styles 61
CHAPTER FIVE: What about Socialising? 69
   Socialising in theory 69
   Socialising in practice 74

CHAPTER SIX: Parenting while Home Educating ... 81
    Parenting theories...81
Epilogue to Part One 91
    Pros and cons 91

Part Two

Prologue to Part Two 99
    Home Education and Subjects........................99
CHAPTER SEVEN: Maths................................ 103
    Maths for younger children 103
    Maths for older children............................. 109
CHAPTER EIGHT: Reading and Writing 115
CHAPTER NINE: Other Subjects 131
    Science... 131
    Humanities 138
    Other subjects 145
CHAPTER TEN: Exams and University 155
    GCSEs and A-levels 155
    Applying for university 160
Epilogue: Our Home Education Journey 165
    The primary years.................................... 165
    The secondary years 172
References 183
Acknowledgements 189

Preface

This book has been a long time in its gestation. It began as a small experimental website, back in February 1999. We had been home educating for a little over a year, in the early days of the Internet. Although there were many good sites for homeschoolers in the United States, there were almost none for the British equivalent.

I found personal sites with links to resources — mostly American — and a few pages that talked about different families' experiences. But most of the information about home education in general was hard to find. Most of my knowledge about the topic came from an excellent online forum which I joined. I asked basic questions, and was given useful replies.

We were only originally planning to home educate for a year while we settled into a new environment. In the early months, I was sure that school was intrinsically superior to home education. I was under the misapprehension that structure and curricula were important to enable a child to learn efficiently. I believed, too, that parents taking on the role of teachers needed to be authoritative: to create clear boundaries in their homes, to determine what should be taught.

Essentially I thought that the role of a home educator was to impart knowledge to children in conjunction with the country's national curriculum. I didn't feel equipped to do this at all, as my natural style of parenting is more relaxed. But I felt that it was the right thing to do. On the forum, I argued the case quite forcefully at times.

I am thankful that most of the long-term home educators with whom I interacted remained calm and patient. I was guided through the concepts of lifelong learning; of self-directed, autonomous education. I learned about the importance of trusting children to find their own paths and to ask the right questions. I am still grateful to the participants of the forum who encouraged me to continue the journey with a lot more confidence and freedom.

At the same time, I also learned about a few of the problems which some children, particularly teenagers, can experience in secondary schools. I had not, until then, understood how privileged I had been as a teenager. I attended an all-girls' grammar school in the 1970s, where there was some excellent teaching and very little bullying. On the whole I liked my school days, although it was surprising to realise, twenty years later, how little I remembered of subjects in which I had gained good O-level results.

I had to go through my own de-schooling period. As a writer, I turned my new understanding and knowledge into articles which I hoped would be of use to other home educators. After starting my own site, on the now defunct Geocities platform, I wrote for commercial sites, too. I produced articles which — as the other sites petered away — were gradually transferred to my site. Inevitably there was some duplication, but that did not matter; I realised even then that nobody reads through an entire site.

Preface

In the meantime, other UK home educating sites started, and mine became less significant. But by that stage I was hooked on this way of writing online. I re-designed my site several times, over the years. I added new pages now and again. I bought a domain, updated it, lost interest for a while, went back to it...

All the time, in the back of my mind, were comments from some of my site visitors who said that I should make it into a book. That was not something I felt able to do while involved in home educating. Besides, I had no clue how to start. It seemed like such a daunting idea that I put it off for many years.

But the thought would not go away. Eventually I tried writing a rough outline and started putting the material into book form, only to lose track of where I was. Then self-doubt crept in, and I would wonder why I was reinventing the wheel. There are, after all, many good books on the topic of home education already.

By the second half of 2014, the idea was nagging too much in my brain to be forgotten. New software, Scrivener, made the book-writing process easier. I imported the entire site and rearranged it into a book format. I then spent many hours removing duplications and altering outdated information. I also removed all the pages of links to other resources, as I knew those would not work in a book.

Then I spent more time procrastinating. During 2015 I did very little on the project. During the early part of 2016 I set to work, a little at a time, to edit thoroughly and proof-read. I was still doing so at the start of 2017. I did random bits and pieces off and on through the rest of that year, and finally, January 2018, decided I had to finish it. I did quite a bit of editing that month, then put it aside until October 2018.

Self-publishing via 'print on demand' has become much easier; my husband has produced books for himself and others via this technology, and we know it can work for this book. My aim is to publish at the start of February 2019, on the twentieth anniversary of the site — so, last-minute as ever, I am finalising the text in January 2019.

It has been an interesting process, and I hope the result is roughly what people hoped for when they asked me to produce a 'book of the site'. The site — http://home-ed.info — has far more content including links to online educational resources, curriculum providers, and articles about parenting. There are, in addition, many more pages on the site about maths and grammar than I have included in this book, and some specifically educational pages about other topics which interest me. But they are not relevant to this book, which has turned into a general low-key introduction to home education for those considering it as an option, or just starting.

What remains in this book, then, is a summary of what I learned about educating children at home, and about parenting 'free range' children. I have tried to be as open-minded and flexible as possible; as I state, more than once, every child and each family is different. I have kept the legalities to a minimum as they are covered extensively in other books and websites. The information and suggestions in this book are interspersed with personal anecdotes which, I hope, give useful examples.

Above all, this book is about sharing our lives as a former home educating family. Inevitably our journey included some wrong turnings, and several detours. There were many occasions when we had not the faintest idea what we were doing. But I hope it will provide some hope and encouragement to anyone who is feeling full of trepidation as they embark on this adventure.

Structure of the book

The book is in two sections. The first is about home education itself, for people who are considering the possibility, or who are being asked difficult questions about it. There is a brief explanation of the de-registration procedure, followed by some suggested ways to embark on home education. Other chapters consider the pros and cons of home education, what we mean by 'successful', and the ways different children are motivated — or not.

The first section of the book also explains some of the reasons why so many families choose home education. It attempts to answer some questions, many of which I asked myself when we first came across the idea, such as:

- Why would anyone keep their children at home all day?
- How can parents teach all that qualified teachers can?
- What is education anyway?
- What are our children missing out on when they are home educated?

A prevailing myth is that home educators are socially awkward or even downright antisocial; this is far from true. So there is a section about the social side of home education. This is based partly on research and also on our own experience. I hope it should allay any concerns you might have. Some of the first section includes some concepts which are as much to do with relaxed parenting in general as home education.

Part Two briefly looks at different subjects which are studied in school, and some possible ways to cover them when home educating, particularly if you have young children. If you are in the UK, you are not required to do this, and you can ignore the second section entirely if you prefer. Nonetheless, many home educators, particularly at first, try to cover the core of what is studied in schools. This section of the book should guide you in suitable directions if you and your children want to do that. The section ends with a chapter about public exams (which, again, are optional) and applying for sixth form college or university, for those who wish to do so.

Most of the chapters in Part One end with a few paragraphs about our own relevant experiences, for those who prefer a more personal touch. There is also an epilogue to the book which recounts, in far more detail, our own adventures with home education and a brief summary of what our sons did afterwards.

Feel free to dip into this book, to browse, to jot down notes in the margins, and to discuss it with friends. If you want to get in touch with me, to ask questions, to point out errors, or even to disagree, please do so through the website home-ed.info where the idea for this book first germinated, or via the related Facebook page.

A note about pronouns

When I started writing articles for my website, I often referred to my own experiences. Both my children are boys, and I found myself using the pronoun 'he' even when writing about a child in general. Since I grew up with the understanding that the pronoun 'he' could mean 'he or she', I did not worry about it.

When editing for this book form, in an era where pronouns have become controversial, I have pluralised 'child' to 'children' where possible. But there are also places where I have used the words 'they' or 'their' when referring to a child In the singular. I find this usage a bit

Preface

awkward, but it is the officially correct gender-neutral term.

There may still be places where the pronoun 'he' has crept into this book, without referring to a specific person. If so, please understand it as intended, with the old-fashioned meaning of 'he or she'. I am writing about children and their education, not their gender, their orientation, or anything else that separates them.

Part One

Her method of education was very much ahead of her time, for she employed the modern method of self-government, and allowed her pupils to study whatever subject they felt most drawn to at the moment.

Elizabeth Goudge, *A City of Bells*

CHAPTER ONE
Why home educate?

Legalities in brief

Home education — sometimes called 'homeschooling' — is legal in most English-speaking countries of the world, and in many others too. Some countries have specific requirements, some expect annual reporting or resting, and the laws change from time to time. In the United States, each individual state has its own rules. If you are considering home education, it is important to check the laws of your country or state, and to keep up to date with any changes that may be made.

The UK, at the time of writing, is still the place where it is easiest to educate children at home, free of any specific requirements. So that is the focus of this book. But most of the content is relevant to any parents hoping to educate their children at home, or to supplement their learning if the children are in school.

According to the 1996 Education Act in England and Wales, parents are responsible for providing their children's education 'at school or otherwise'. The Act states that education, whatever form it takes, must be suitable for the age, ability and aptitude of each child. The same wording is used in Northern Ireland. Scottish law is a little different; the Scottish Education Act states that, 'every child has a right to an education, and it is the duty of the parent of every school age child to provide that education, either by sending the child to school, or by other means.'

So UK law says clearly that it is up to parents, not the state, to ensure that children receive appropriate education.

That realisation can be a turning point. The UK, unlike some other countries, still officially recognises the primacy of family life. A child's education is not the responsibility of the government, the local education authority, or even the schools. It is the responsibility of the parents.

What this means in practice will vary from child to child. There are many good schools that can provide a useful education which suits some individuals well. However, parents should ensure that this is the case. To send a child to school is the usual choice, meaning that parents are delegating part of their educational responsibility. That's fine, if it works well. But it is not a requirement. If a chosen school fails to deliver an appropriate education to any child, it is ultimately the responsibility of the child's parents to do something about it.

Parents in the UK who prefer, for whatever reason, to educate their children outside a school environment do not have to be trained teachers. Nor do they need any specific qualifications. They do not have to follow a curriculum, they are not required to teach any particular subjects, and the children do not have to take tests or exams. The law simply states, and it's worth repeating, that education, however delivered or transmitted, must be suitable for the age, ability and aptitude of each child. Some home educating families choose to use a curriculum, or to think about discrete subjects, and some opt for exams such as GCSEs. But none of these is essential.

You can find more details about the current laws on the relevant government websites, or those of local authorities.

Why home educate?

If you have toddlers or children who have not yet reached the compulsory education age, you may feel pressurised into looking at local schools. Applications for popular schools have to be made almost as soon as a child is born. Families move house, sometimes, simply to be in the catchment area for a school they like. Children are enrolled, younger and younger, at pre-school groups and nurseries.

If this suits your child then it is not a problem. But some children are not ready to move away from their parents (or other carers) at the age of three or four. That does not make them 'clingy' or emotionally immature. It is healthy for children to be happily attached to their home and family. Schooling has only been the default option for about a hundred and twenty years, and in some countries even now, formal education does not begin until a child is six or seven years old.

Parental instincts are usually sound. If you feel that your four-year-old would benefit from an extra year or two at home, then home educating may be the best choice. If you do not feel comfortable with the local schools when you visit them, that would be another good reason to home educate. You can review your options each year. Home educated children usually find it easy to adjust to a school environment if circumstances change, or if they and their parents decide that they would benefit from being in a classroom.

There are some families whose lifestyle is relaxed and flexible, and who do not want to be limited by the hours and dates of school terms. They may opt to educate their children at home because they feel philosophically that it suits their way of life. There are also those, sometimes of strong religious affiliations, who feel that children are indoctrinated in schools. They prefer to teach their own beliefs at home rather than seeing their children mix with those who might challenge them.

If your children are older, they may already be in school. If they like it, and if you are happy about their school environment, its general atmosphere, and the ways they are learning, then there is probably no reason to consider any alternative. School classrooms have become the default places to educate children in most of the world. For some children and teenagers, school can be a great place to learn and develop new skills and interests.

However, not every child is temperamentally suited to a classroom, nor to structured learning. Many children and teens are bored or frustrated in school, and stressed by the number of tests that modern children are required to take. Real learning suffers while children are coached to pass yet another exam, or to achieve a government-mandated target that does not necessarily tie in with their own learning styles or interests.

Even in the primary years there are some children who struggle, sometimes in vain, to understand what they are taught in the classroom. A minority may have specific learning difficulties which could be helped by diagnosis and professional advice. But some children are not wired to learn well from books or organised lessons. Not all children can — or should — sit still for lengthy periods. Many are active, hands-on learners who find it difficult to absorb anything in a structured classroom environment.

Moreover, twenty-five or thirty children of the same age are unlikely to learn in the same way, at the same time, and at the same rate. This is why most schools in the UK have ability groups and other forms of differentiation; where possible, they also have extra assistants or volunteers within each class. But no matter how good the school, a classroom teacher's job is a challenging one. It is more so nowadays than it used to be, with increased regulations, paperwork, required tests and targets. That means that there is less time for individual attention to each of the pupils. There is also very little time to encourage creative thinking or tangential learning that may go in a different direction from a planned lesson.

Then there are children who are badly hurt by teasing, or by feeling incompetent. Some, wanting to fit in with their peers, resort to rebellion in their teens. If the subjects taught at school do not inspire them, they may become bored and potentially aggressive. Sometimes students who want to be popular with their peers are dragged into trouble by others.

Perhaps none of this applies to you or your children. But if you or they are in any way dissatisfied with their schools, or if you move away and are not impressed with what is available in your new district, you may want to consider the alternative: to educate them, at least for a year or two, out of school.

Attitudes to schools

When we have passionate beliefs, we sometimes want to condemn those who believe or behave differently. Examples are easy to find. Politics can divide close friends or families, each side convinced that their philosophy is correct. People of one religion — or one group within a religion — often condemn those who believe anything different. Vegetarians and vegans can be extremely negative about meat-eaters, and the reverse is also often true.

Inevitably, the choices we make for our children arouse strong feelings. When we have made a decision, it can be easy to assume it is one that everyone else should take too. It starts when we decide what pain relief — if any — to have when giving birth, and whether we plan to go to hospital or stay at home. Battles are fought over whether we breast-feed or bottle-feed, and how long to continue. It doesn't get better. Parents criticise each other over how they dress and feed their children, how their days are structured (or not), and, relevant to this book, how they choose to educate them.

As a former home educator, it is easy for me to see positive things in home education and to gloss over problems. It is also natural for those who believe in the school system to find good things about classrooms, and to condemn home education. This might be based on hearsay, or it could be from having met one or two families whose children, they feel, were not adequately educated at home.

Looking back from the perspective of late middle age, I realise that many of these things are far less important than they seemed to be when I was going through them. When I meet a young adult, I have no idea whether they were born by Caesarian section, whether they were bottle-fed from birth, whether they were 'free range' or structured in their home lives. Neither can I necessarily tell whether they went to school or not.

It is undeniable that there are some children who have been so damaged by their school experiences that they and their parents cannot see anything positive about schools. But that does not mean that all home educators are anti-school. A few teachers are harsh, or choose favourites in their classes. But it does not follow that all school teachers should be condemned because of a poor experience with one of them.

Inevitably, we make mistakes as parents. We base our decisions on current circumstances, on our preconceived ideas, on what we have read, and on what we observe. Sometimes we change our minds as the children grow up. We do not always listen to advice, because we already have our own values and beliefs. At times we are too tired or stressed to make good choices. Still, the majority of parents care deeply for their children and want what is best for them.

Each child is a unique individual. Nobody can be certain how they would feel if they were in a different situation, with a different child, in another location and with another family's needs. So before going further with this book, I want to put aside the negative stereotypes about both schools and home educators, and attempt to consider the subject in a balanced way.

I am always glad to hear of positive school experiences. On the whole I liked school, and my sons also enjoyed most of their time at school before we moved abroad. One of them is now a school teacher himself. The system is not perfect, but neither are any families. Most teachers are hard-working and dedicated, and do the best they can for the pupils in their care. A good school can foster a sense of community, and some lifelong friendships can be formed alongside a love of learning.

My first philosophical leap was from thinking, 'What are my children missing by not being in school?' to, 'What are they gaining by not being in school?' But I was still seeing school as the default. I had to move further, to thinking, 'It is irrelevant what might have been different if circumstances were otherwise. So what can I do for my children now, in their current situation?'

Nowadays, many years after my sons left home, I think of school as one option for part of a child's education, on a par with music lessons, drama, sports clubs and so on. Some children love sports and want to be on every team they can find. Others don't like team sports at all. Some children thrive in school education, some thrive at home. No child can take advantage of every activity available, so let's pick and choose carefully, depending on the children's interests and abilities as well as their personalities.

Some schools are better (and more conducive to learning) than others. Some children are far more suited to a school environment than others. Some home educating families thrive, some children are not so happy being educated at home. The important thing is that (at least in the UK, as well as some other countries) there is a choice. We have no need to criticise those who make a different decision. Parenting is hard enough without condemnation from other parents. So in my view it is best to live amicably alongside each other, no matter how our neighbours choose to fulfil their responsibility for their children's education.

If we are secure in our belief that we have chosen what is best for us, we should allow others the freedom to make different decisions. Let's stand together as parents, whether our children are in school or not. We need to proclaim the freedom of choice in education, so that each family can choose how best to satisfy their children's educational needs.

Benefits of home education

If you have toddlers or young children and are undecided about how to educate them, it is a good idea to visit the schools in your area to see what they are like, and how they function. You should have the opportunity to ask questions about their facilities and philosophies. It is also helpful to speak to parents who have children at the schools, and, if possible, to some of the children who are already attending.

Take your child with you when you visit, and see what their reaction is. Does the prospect of school seem exciting, perhaps because they have friends there? Do the classrooms look like enjoyable places to be, or are they daunting and scary? Is there anything that they offer that you could not provide at home?

A shy child will not be made braver by being forced into a group environment before being ready. It is a strange (and untrue) myth that children can only learn to socialise when they are in school. Four is a very young age for a child to be in full-time classroom education. So some parents decide to educate their children at home for the first few years only, to give them a bit more maturity before entering a structured environment.

There are also increasing numbers of parents who home educate their children by preference, without ever seriously considering sending them to school.

Some immediate benefits of home education are:
- A clear understanding of what and how a child is learning

- The ability to work as and when the child is most motivated
- A child can learn in his own way, at his own pace
- No early morning rushes, uniform, or lunch money
- The possibility of off-peak holidays

Remember that no decision is final. If you educate your child at home for a while, you can always consider using a school at some later point.

So, why home educate? Let me turn the question around and ask, 'Why NOT home educate?' Schools may have become the default place to educate most children, but in the long-term view of history, mass education is a fairly new idea. Successive governments call for reforms, changes to the curriculum and different guidelines for teachers. Classroom education is not guaranteed to be successful. School pupils are, essentially, guinea pigs for whatever is the current trend in educational theory.

It is true that many children and teenagers do well in a school environment, emerging with useful qualifications and a wide range of knowledge. But there are also those who drop out, or turn to drugs or violence because they are so frustrated.

It is arguable that bright children within a positive family environment will do well wherever they are educated. If your child is happy to learn in a group setting in a structured way, and if the school atmosphere is friendly, with flexible staff and good relationships with parents, then you and your child may decide that school is a good idea. Even so, it is good to think of it as a deliberate choice, one that may be changed, rather than as the automatic default for thirteen years.

Our experience

Our family did not start home education for any idealistic motivations. We had no idea that it was a positive option, or that so many children do not go to school.

However, we moved from the UK to Cyprus when our sons were eleven and nine. English-speaking schools were expensive. We decided — reluctantly — to educate the boys at home for the rest of the academic year, and look into the available options during that time.

I had no good reasons, no philosophy of life that fit with home education. I was persuaded that it would 'do no harm', but was convinced I would not be able to continue beyond the primary education years.

I have written more about the early part of our journey in the epilogue to the book. Suffice it to say that we soon discovered many practical benefits to family life, with the flexibility to take time off when we had visitors, and to travel outside of school holidays. Our sons flourished, and I found the experience of home education far more rewarding than I had expected.

CHAPTER TWO
How to home educate (in theory)

Parents as educators

How can untrained parents educate their children? This was perhaps the most important question for me when we embarked on home education, even though we thought that it was just a temporary measure.

I was reminded by people on an online home education forum that, in their first few years of life, our children learn an entire language; sometimes more than one. Untrained and often nervous parents succeed in introducing their offspring to the world. They meet dozens of people, they experience different situations and places, and we probably read our babies and toddlers hundreds of books.

By the time they are three or four years old, our children know how to dress themselves, how to eat a variety of foods, how to use the toilet... and they learned all these things without any direct 'teaching'. They develop with great rapidity from helpless dependent babies into small people with minds of their own, who continually ask questions and have a great hunger for learning.

If you have an inquisitive child, you may feel that you cannot possibly answer all their questions. This may seem a bit worrying if your child is still a toddler! But there is no guarantee that your child's interests would be fostered or his questions answered in a school environment. Teachers nowadays have little time for questions unrelated to the National Curriculum.

As a parent, you may not have all the specialist knowledge of a trained teacher. But you have more time to research: to go to the library, to ask friends, or to browse the Internet with your children. If they want to know about a particular country, for instance, or to learn about electricity, or to make pots with clay, or anything else that takes his interest, then you can follow it up together. If you are ignorant on the topic, you can learn alongside each other, rather than being limited to a curriculum or timeframe.

It was part of my own de-schooling process to realise that life is not divided into discrete subjects. Topics arise naturally as part of conversation, perhaps after reading books or listening to the news. As we meet other people, our horizons expand. Ethical, philosophical and sociological issues come up in conversation with people of all ages, as we discover that different people see the world in a variety of ways.

If a topic is of interest to your children, then they will want to find out more. If it is of no interest to them, and if it does not come up naturally in conversation, then it is not necessary to insist that they learn about it. I

How to home educate (in theory)

have forgotten the majority of the physics I learned at secondary school. Has it mattered? Not in the slightest.

As for day-to-day learning, I doubt if there are any two home educating families who follow the exact same routine. Some like to use a structured curriculum. Some like to make timetables of different subjects and study them regularly, as if they are in school. Some prefer an informal, interest-led approach with flexible timescales. Some families do not separate education from life at all. Some adapt their approach from week to week, depending on circumstances.

If you want to use school-type textbooks, there is a wide variety available, updated regularly. If you browse your local bookshop you should see a reasonable selection. For a less expensive option, searching on the Internet will reveal thousands of pages of information on any topic, sometimes with games, interactive quizzes, or ideas for projects. Your library is another useful source: you will find books on most topics, DVDs and sometimes computer software or applications to borrow.

Whether your approach is formal or not, you will find that learning experiences come from all kinds of sources, not just books and computers. When reading and conversation are natural parts of daily life, rather than rushed through in evenings and weekends, your child will learn in a relaxed way, at his own pace, when he is ready to do so. More importantly, topics and subjects taught in schools are only a tiny part of the broader concept of 'education'.

You do not need to know everything in advance. As your children grow up, you can learn alongside them. Home education can be a lifelong process, as you explore the world, discuss theories, try out new crafts and discover new ideas. So long as children and teens know how to find things out, and what questions to ask, there is no boundary to their learning at any stage of their lives.

Our experience

My background is in maths and computer programming. I did A-levels in maths, further maths and Ancient Greek (yes, a slightly odd combination!) and a degree in maths, with a focus on programming languages. I then worked for some years as a programmer for a large organisation before stopping work to have children.

I am also an extensive reader, and since childhood have been a writer. I'm one of those people who can spell naturally, and am aware of correct grammatical structures. English and languages were my strengths, along with maths, at school.

On the other hand, I disliked most sciences, geography and history when I was at school. I gave them all up as soon as I could. My general knowledge is pitiful, my understanding of politics minimal. I am not musical or artistic, and I have never liked team sports of any kind, although I have always enjoyed dancing.

My husband did science A-levels and then started a career which included significant training which has made him highly competent in many aspects of physics including electronics, sound engineering and lighting design. He is also far more aware of geography and politics than I am.

So in theory we could cover most school topics, although neither of us has any training in teaching. In practice, I was the one responsible for home education, as he was working full-time. When we started home educating, we assumed that our sons would go back to school after about a year. It was possible that we would return to the UK a year later, and it still hadn't occurred to us that we might continue home educating there.

We used some maths and English books recommended by the boys' UK school when we started. We borrowed a French course, and a Greek one, on cassette tapes and we visited the local thrift store, and some church bazaars to pick up other 'educational' books. Someone gave us an electronics kit, and we bought a chemistry set. We bought several educational CD-Roms, too. Some of these proved useful, to a limited extent, but many were unnecessary. Slowly — imperceptibly — we began to relax into home education, in our own way, according to our own styles.

Is home education time-consuming?

In the UK there are no requirements or restrictions related to the time taken for home education, or for the topics to be studied. The law simply states that education must be suitable for the child's age, ability and aptitude. What that means is open to individual interpretation. Each family needs to determine how to make this work for their particular children.

One concern I have heard when people consider home education is that it must be extremely time-consuming. According to people I have corresponded with online, some officials, unaware of the law, have been known to suggest that four or five hours every day should be spent on 'schoolwork'. Yet for young children, learning at their own pace, this is an excessive amount, which can lead to burnout. Moreover, it would leave little time for the self-directed learning which is such an important feature of home education.

Before we started home educating, I imagined that we would work in set periods, much like happens a school classroom. However, my sons calculated that, at least at primary school, there is a surprisingly small amount of academic 'work' done in any school day. Although they spent six and a half hours at school each day, around two hours were for lunchtime and breaks, including lining up, hanging up coats and so on. Then about half an hour was spent on registration and Assemblies every morning.

So only four hours were spent in classrooms or working with teachers. Of those four hours, around an hour per day was spent on PE, art or music. These are an important part of education, but we knew that they were not subjects I could help my sons with. So we had already decided that they would doing them at other times, perhaps with outside instructors.

Thus in each school day about three hours was spent on academic subjects. During this time, in the course of each week, they covered maths, English, science, religious education, information technology, history and geography. Each day was divided into periods of 35-40 minutes.

My sons then pointed out that in each forty-minute 'lesson' there were at least five minutes at the beginning where children put away books from previous lessons, and the teacher handed out exercise books or paper. Then there would typically be five minutes or so of class discussion about the topic on hand. In that time, the teacher would remind the pupils what they did the previous day (or week), and would ask a few guided questions.

They would then brainstorm into the current lesson. My sons liked this, but said that only a few children in each class participated in such sessions. As I had volunteered in other classes myself, I realised they were right. In a typical lesson, the introduction would be followed

How to home educate (in theory)

by about five minutes of direct 'teaching'. The teacher would explain what the class was expected to learn, building on previous lessons. They would give examples, and would often ask more questions to encourage the children to think for themselves.

After that, there would be a few more minutes as the teacher explained the assignment to be attempted during that session. This might be an exercise from a book, or a worksheet, or some creative writing. In a science lesson it might be conducting an experiment in groups. After the explanation, the children would take another couple of minutes drawing margins, writing the date, and ensuring they had spelled the title of the assignment correctly.

Finally there would be ten to fifteen minutes at most while the children attempted the assigned work. The teacher would move around the class to encourage children, correct mistakes where relevant, and answer questions.

For children who like structure, and whose aptitude and ability match the level of teaching, this style of classroom teaching can be a good learning experience. For those who are further ahead academically, however, the pace can feel frustrating and boring. For others, who may not be ready, yet, for this particular topic or level of learning, a lesson of this kind can be confusing and discouraging.

More relevant to us, as we thought about home education, was realising that even in the best scenario there were no more than twenty minutes of real 'education' in any lesson period. So on a typical school day there is around an hour and a half of real learning. That assumes a motivated and interested child who is receptive to the topics covered, as well as an inspiring teacher.

At secondary level (11-16) there is inevitably more focussed educational time. Students learn to work better on their own as they mature, and are grouped so that there is less disparity of ability within a class. Even then, there are rarely more than three hours per day of academics in total.

As we progressed through our home education journey, I found myself thinking less in terms of focussed teaching or bookwork. Even an hour and a half was too much, some days, for academic learning. I gradually realised that the whole of life is educational. Children might ask questions as they wake up, or as they are saying goodnight. They may want to spend a lot of time researching in libraries or online. You may find yourself travelling a long way to visit historic sites to encourage their interest in their chosen topics. If you are reading an interesting book together, you might spend several hours at a time with it.

If you are considering home education, it can be worthwhile to write down what you and your children do on any typical day (at the weekend or in holiday time, if they are currently going to school). Note down any questions they ask, and keep track of any time you read to them. Also make note of time spent together cooking, sorting laundry, going for walks and so on. You will probably find that there are many educational opportunities unrelated to text-books or school 'subjects', which are just as important, if not more so.

Boredom is not conducive to learning, and many children are not wired to learn in set periods of time each day. They tend to learn best when they are interested in something. When that happens, they are likely to initiate a discussion or ask questions. Education is about opening doors and helping children to know how to learn and to do their own research. It is not about performing set assignments or learning by heart. Nor is it necessary to have specific 'educational' parts of the day.

So, is home education time consuming? Yes — and no. It is full-time and all consuming, in the sense that you may be asked anything at any time. At least when your children are young, you must be continually willing to enable, to discuss, to answer questions, and perhaps to mediate in arguments. But this kind of thing does not happen all the time. When your children are motivated, they will probably spend hours on their own playing, or reading, or learning in ways that suit their personalities best, without any real need for supervision. In terms of hours, home education is far less time-consuming than a full-time paid job.

Our experience

Despite agreeing that an hour and a half was the learning time in a typical school day, we were quite ambitious when we started. We decided to allocate about three hours in all to our home education each weekday morning, from around 9.30 to 12.30 with a break in the middle. We soon found that this was too much. We cut down to four days a week, and it was still too much. We made it a lot more flexible, time-wise, and it was still too much.

At first I spent time making worksheets or reading through material in evenings, to be sure that I knew what we would do the next day. But after the first few months I found this to be unnecessary. When we acquired a new text-book, I would skim through to see what topics were covered, but found it much better to approach home education fresh each day, and decide with my sons what they would like to do.

On a 'good' day (while I was still thinking in a school-like way) we would spend less than two hours on academics, including lots of discussion and veering off at tangents. My sons would sometimes work on examples from their maths textbooks on paper, but only those which they needed to do to ensure that they had understood the current topic. Their creative written work (usually typed) included letters, web pages, and stories for competitions in magazines.

Gradually we would move away from any kind of structure, and that worked well when they were involved in projects, or reading interesting books. But from time to time, we worried that we were doing almost nothing overtly educational. So we made ourselves a new timetable for a while. But somehow we never managed to stick to them for long.

When they were teenagers, as explained further in the epilogue, we started using a curriculum for part of their education. Even after we started that, we found that about two hours per day was more than sufficient for the coursework. We often spent another hour or so reading and discussing other topics together. We continued taking breaks, or days off, as seemed appropriate and still managed to cover everything we intended to.

So yes, it was a significant time commitment. But totally worthwhile. Some parents manage to combine home education with self-employment, working at home. Others work part-time and share the children's education and care with a partner or grandparent. I am not that organised. I could not have done it if I had been career-minded, or if I had not enjoyed spending time with my sons as a full-time mother. I was available from first thing in the morning until night-time, if I was needed. But I never felt that it was too time-consuming.

Motivation

In schools, children have little choice but to follow the system of timetabling, specific subjects, planned curriculum, set assignments and so on. These are necessary for efficiency in the classroom. A school is a structured organisation, where — at least in theory — one teacher can enable learning for around thirty children of similar age.

For some of these children, timetabled teaching of this kind may fit their learning requirements well. Perhaps they are motivated to work hard and complete their assignments because they appreciate step-by-step learning and reinforcement. Some may enjoy the challenge of homework or writing assignments, and find satisfaction in their feelings of progress and of grasping new concepts or facts.

But this is not always the case. For some children in school, their only motivation to do anything is to please the teacher, or to get good marks for the sake of their parents. For those who are competitive, the motivation may be to beat other children for first place in the class. Unfortunately, pleasing and competing teach children that learning is not in itself worthwhile unless there is some kind of 'reward' at the end. When parents offer their children money or gifts for getting good results, they are reinforcing this negative kind of motivation.

Moreover, there are also some children for whom there is almost no motivation to learn in the classroom. If they struggle to understand and feel shame when they ask questions, they may give up entirely. If they are stressed due to bullying, or indeed if they are bored and unchallenged, they may do minimal work and make almost no progress. Some see nothing ahead but years of tedium, and may have no ambition or plans for life after school.

Home education gives an entirely different environment for learning. Children can be free to follow their own interests, and to find their own motivation. For parents considering home education, this can seem rather concerning. We are conditioned to believe that there are things that children 'ought' to know, or that they have to be kept on track with a curriculum. Some people wonder how children can be motivated to do anything without some kind of outside pressure or external reward.

Think back to when your children were toddlers. They did not need external motivation to learn to talk. The drive to speak was built into them; communication with parents was its own reward. Nor did they need any direct encouragement to learn to crawl, and then to walk. When they tried to explore and climb, they might have been discouraged at times, but that did not stop them. They learned to feed themselves, to build with bricks, to throw balls, and much more.

Perhaps these skills developed with some parental help, but your children did not need any extra reward for their achievements. They gained great satisfaction from being able to do something new. Even quite young toddlers will often spend lengthy periods of trial and error as they strive to master a different skill. The drive to learn and achieve is innate.

Moving beyond the toddler years, a young child's 'reward' for asking questions is finding out more knowledge, and gaining a better understanding of how the world works. I doubt if you gave him stars on a chart for the number of questions he asked. Learning was his delight. The boundary between play and education did not exist as far as he was concerned.

Sadly, some children find their natural curiosity curbed by schools. This is not the fault of the teachers:

they must teach to a government-approved curriculum. One teacher, no matter how skilled, cannot possibly answer thirty children's questions on random topics. In some cases they have no time to expand on the day's planned lessons, even if a child asks a relevant question. So, gradually, children in school learn to comply, as far as they can, with what they are being taught. They stop asking other kinds of questions. This works quite well for some, particularly if they have sufficient energy to ask their questions at home. But for others it is de-motivating, and not conducive to learning.

When children are educated at home, they tend to retain their initial love of learning. If they keep the desire to find out more, they will still experience the enjoyment of discovery and the satisfaction of understanding something new. Their motivation is from within; their learning is still its own reward. When they are free to follow their interests, and encouraged to keep asking questions, they will have no shame about asking when they need to know something. Without the constraints of a timetable and the needs of a class full of children, they can bring up new topics whenever they think about them.

That is not to say that you must be able to answer every question yourself. It is fine for an older child to be pointed in the direction of encyclopaedias or the Internet. Alternatively you could suggest appropriate books to read, if a question requires more than a simple answer, or seems to be showing a deeper interest than can be fulfilled by a paragraph or two online.

An older child should be able to wait for an answer if the parent is busy with something else. But it is crucial not to let learning moments pass by, whether they happen during a weekday morning, or late on a Saturday night. A child who really wants to learn something can do so much more quickly and effectively than a child who has to fit in with a curriculum.

Part of the reason for lack of achievement, sometimes, is fear of failure. Children often produce the minimum they can get away with at school, and don't like to try anything more complicated in case they make mistakes.

This is not an inherent problem with schools. One teacher I spoke to said that he would always encourage 'wrong' and creative-type comments in a classroom discussion, because people need to learn from mistakes. He encouraged children to see that a 'wrong' answer may be the route to a new and better one than the simplest, most obvious response. But he also said that many children were frightened of making mistakes or saying something silly. Sometimes that was because other teachers may reject 'wrong' answers, or classmates might ridicule them. Any of these problems might lead a shy child to give up offering answers or thinking for himself.

Home educated children can be free from false expectations from anyone, and free from competition with their peers. They are much more able to get on and learn in the way that suits them best. But home educating parents need to be patient with 'wrong' answers, and not demean or tease a child who makes mistakes.

When a child has spent the pre-teen years discovering the joy of learning, free to ask questions and to follow his own interests entirely, it is a natural step to realising that some interests require depth of study which may be tedious, or difficult. Parents should never push their children into study. Having said that, some children want reminders or may ask for help in making plans for assignments or revision for courses with a time-limit.

At some point your child may decide that qualifications are important. If that happens, it is best to take this desire seriously. It can be constructive to discuss possible careers with your child, and ways of achieving the qualifications he might need. Some home educated children go to school for a few years in their teens to gain GCSEs or A-levels. Others use correspondence courses, or take classes at local colleges or adult education centres.

Others begin a volunteer post or job which turns into a full-time position. Some develop a creative skill such as writing or photography or web design, and build up their own careers. Some discover that work experience is more valuable than qualifications and may start an apprenticeship. Others may decide to take a degree course by correspondence, or to go to a vocational college where a portfolio of work is of more value than any qualifications. What is important is that the motivation to learn, and — perhaps — to take formal exams should come from the child.

Not all work is enjoyable. It could be that your child decides on a course of study, as preparation for a future career, and quickly becomes bored or frustrated. But if the motivation has come from within, there should be a goal to aim for. Unless there are serious problems, your child will probably work through the boredom for the sake of the eventual goal. This can be good preparation for adult life, when they may frequently need to do chores or work which are not innately appealing — such as laundry — in order to gain something for which they are motivated, such as clean clothes.

On the other hand, if a course turns out to be a disaster, a home educated child, motivated from within, should feel able to quit and try something else. Without the need to please others, it is easier to balance the pros and cons of continuing something which one does not enjoy.

Many adults work for external motivation such as a paycheque. There is no reason why our teenage children should not, at times, agree to do particular jobs such as babysitting or mowing the lawn, for which they are paid. They should, of course, expect to take a normal part in family life and chores, appropriate to age, without payment or other reward. But if there are jobs which we might pay someone else to do, a child should be free to take up the employment opportunity if they are capable and willing.

If they can find paid work which they also enjoy, so much the better; this is good experience preparing them for the world of work. As children grow up they will inevitably find times when motivation is at least partly from outside. But it is good to be aware of every opportunity to encourage children's internal motivation, and to help them to see education and learning as an exciting, life-long adventure.

Our experience

The things my sons really wanted to do were the things they became most excited about. Whether writing a novel, or playing a new computer game, or reading a favourite book, they would, if sufficiently motivated, pursue it for hours at a time. When they were interested in a new topic, they would ask questions and research. They learned from mistakes, and often pushed the boundaries of their understanding a long way beyond mine.

When my older son was fourteen, he thought he wanted to be a graphic designer or programmer. I could see that he was following a constructive path in teaching himself about these topics. He was dedicated to what he did, too. He knew how to learn, and how to find out more, and where to look for information on the Internet if he needed to.

By that stage, I had relaxed sufficiently that I was able to trust his judgement, and not worry about the things he wasn't studying. If at some point he suddenly decided he would like to be — for instance — a doctor, then I knew that he would need to take courses in biology and chemistry. Up to that stage, we had only touched on sciences lightly. But if he became motivated towards studying medicine, he would be able to do so because he had found out for himself how to learn.

As he grew older, he taught himself many things and always wanted to know more. He joined theatre classes, and thought for a while about being a professional actor. He taught himself to roller blade and juggle, among other random skills, from books and online.

Our younger son was more structured in his learning, and liked to see achievement in steps. A curriculum worked quite well for him, for basic academics — he was motivated to follow it in order to see progress. He, too, would spend hours reading books, or playing new computer games. He also spent a great deal of time in such diverse topics as learning how to take computers to pieces, teaching himself guitar chords, and baking.

When motivation comes from within, there does not seem to be any limit to our children's learning.

CHAPTER THREE
How to home educate (in practice)

Getting Started

If you have decided that your child would benefit from home education, you may be wondering what you need to do in order to get started. Note that this information is correct at the time of publication, but it is always worth checking the government websites in case any changes to the law have been made. If you are not in the UK, please check the laws of your country, which are likely to be different. If you cannot find out whether home education is legal or not, and what (if any) requirements there may be, you can probably find a relevant group online to ask.

Children who have never been to school

If you live anywhere in the UK, and if your child has never been to school, and if you have not applied for entry at any school, you do not need to do anything in order to start home educating. Since it is your right to choose how to educate your child, you are under no obligation to inform anybody.

If your child is under the age of five, and his name is down for entry at a local school, it would be a good idea to phone the secretary and explain that your arrangements are changing, so that your child's name can be removed. This is a courtesy, not a requirement. You could, after all, have registered at several schools, or you could be moving away. You do not have to explain what other arrangements you are making, but the school will appreciate knowing that they have a space available for another child.

If you have formally accepted a place for your child at a local school, then you should write a letter, informing the school that you no longer require the place. Again, you have no need to let them know that you intend to start home education. 'Making other arrangements' is sufficient. Most good schools have waiting lists and know that there will probably be a few changes before each new school year begins.

If your child has attended a nursery class attached to a school, he may automatically have his name entered on the register for that school. It is important to ensure that his name is removed, if he is not going to go to the school. You do not need to send a formal de-registration letter, as you would if he had already attended school (see below). But you do need to inform the school, in writing, that you do not need the place.

Children already in school

If your children are attending a school, but you plan to educate them at home, then the most important legal requirement is that their names must be removed from the school register. This is so that they are not considered to be truanting. If you live in Scotland, you need permission from your education authority in some cases when your children are in school. You also need permission to de-register if your child is in a special school anywhere within the UK.

If your child is currently in a mainstream school in England, Wales or Northern Ireland, you can de-register by sending a letter to the proprietor (usually the Head). However, you do not need permission to home educate. The letter does not need to be complicated or full of explanations. You do not need to say that you are planning to home educate if you prefer not to. It is your right as a parent to provide education appropriate to your child, so it should be sufficient to state that alternative arrangements are being made for the child's education.

Once the letter is delivered — and if you are not delivering it by hand, it is a good idea to send it by registered post or recorded delivery — the school proprietor should inform the Local Education Authority. You do not have to do so. The Head may then ask you to go into school to discuss your decision. You are not obliged to attend any such meeting, but if you want to stay on good terms with the school it is probably best to agree to a meeting.

It is, obviously, not a good idea to attack the state education system in general, or the school itself. If there have been bullying incidents, or problems with your child's learning, the Head may already be aware that you are considering removing your child. A good Head should encourage you to do what is best for the child. Some may suggest flexi-schooling or another way of continuing to work together.

It will be easier to stay confident if you have drawn up a list of your reasons for home education. It is important to be certain about your decision, but it is also a good idea to remain friendly and not close all doors to a possible future relationship with the school. This is particularly important if you have other children attending the school, or who are likely to do so in future.

According to the experiences of some of my online correspondence, it appears that some school Heads (and, indeed, some LEA officials) are unfamiliar with the relevant parts of the law. This may complicate the process if they ask for details of what you propose to do to educate your child. Questions of this kind can make life more difficult for parents, particularly if they are not, themselves, confident about their legal position. Unfortunately, therefore, de-registration can sometimes be a stressful and lengthy process, although in most cases it should be straightforward.

The important thing, worth repeating, is to ensure that your child's details are removed from the school register if you want to home educate.

Even if the school Head does not challenge your decision, it is likely that, at some point, you will be asked questions about your child's education by a health visitor, or doctor, or by family members. It can be useful to think in advance of some general replies that will not get you involved in a lengthy debate. It is most constructive to express positive reasons for home educating rather than launching into an attack on the problems of classroom education. It can be an excellent opportunity to let people know about the legality of home education, and to give some reasons why you have decided to follow this path.

Remember that it is your legal right to choose how you want your child to be educated. It is not the responsibility of the education authority, or the local school, or, indeed the health visitor. If you are starting with younger children, it may be a good idea to talk about a year at a time, rather than trying to answer difficult questions (which are not yet relevant to you) about the teenage years. No decision about educational methods needs to be final, and it is always a good thing to keep your options open.

Dealing with the Local Education Authority (LEA)

As should now be clear, the UK government officially acknowledges that parents have the right to educate children at home. Thus the LEA has no duties towards a home educated child unless it has evidence that education is not taking place. Nevertheless, as becomes clear from reading any home education forums, some education authorities try to impose regulations.

At some point your LEA is likely to contact you to enquire about the educational provision for your child. This might be within a few days of deregistering, it might be several months later, or it might not happen at all. However it has been established by law that they are entitled to make informal enquiries. It is therefore best for parents to respond courteously to any such enquiries, within reason.

Unfortunately, not all requests from the LEA are reasonable. They might ask you to fill in lengthy questionnaires. They might tell you that you need to teach certain subjects, or to educate at specific times. They might also ask to meet your children within the home environment.

You do not need to reply in detail to any letters from the LEA within the first few months of home education. Children coming out of school need a period of adjustment, or 'de-schooling'. You may need time to establish your educational philosophy, and a pattern to your days. If the LEA contacts you almost immediately, you should be able to tell them that you will respond more fully when you have had a few months to get settled.

Nevertheless, it is a good idea to think about how you would like to deal with the LEA if and when they approach you with a request for information. It is better to be prepared than to become flustered by an unexpected letter or phone call. Remember that they have no right to stop you from educating your child at home, unless they are convinced that no education of any kind is happening.

You may feel comfortable about meeting LEA officers in your home, but you are not obliged to do this. If you are happy to meet them, but prefer not to do so at home, you can arrange another venue; this can be with or without your children. You can invite someone else to the meeting if you wish, such as an experienced local home educator. If you are not comfortable meeting an LEA official at all, you may prefer to write a letter or email explaining your educational philosophy. Some people like meeting strangers and explaining things face-to-face, while others prefer written communication. It is your right to decide how you wish to respond to LEA questions. Every family is different.

Keep in mind that you are not required to follow the National Curriculum or to 'teach' any specific subjects when you are home educating. You do not have to have a room set aside for educational purposes, nor do you need qualifications, or any specific books or other resources.

In theory, there should not be any difficulties or legal problems in choosing to educate your child at home, so long as you ensure that they are NOT registered at a school. Whatever happens, it is best to stay quietly confident about your rights, and to be able to express how you are going to provide education for your children. Rather than arguing with those who disagree with you, focus on what you are doing for your child. If you are uncertain about the long-term future, you can acknowledge, if you wish, that you will take a year at a time and may consider other options in future.

Getting going

After you have made the decision and (if relevant) de-registered your child from school, you may feel at a loss to know what to do. This is normal. Remember that there are no specific rules about home education in the UK. It is up to you and your children to decide how their education is going to work, and what they would like to learn. You do not have to decide in advance; it can be an ongoing process for the whole family.

Starting with young children

If your child is young and has never been to school or any other structured educational environment, then you will not need to do much adjusting. Your child has learned to walk and talk, and to listen to stories and ask questions. Most children, if encouraged to learn in their own style, at their own pace, will absorb information and discover what they need to know from everyday life.

This can feel worrying to those of us who grew up with the standard school model which involves classrooms, curricula and age-related expectations. Yet natural learning has been around for millennia. Individualised education makes more sense than trying to fit thirty or more children into the same mould.

Some families like to mark a child reaching so-called

'compulsory school age', when education is officially required. If that is important to you or to your child, then there are many ways to go about it. You could, for instance, join one of the 'not-back-to-school' picnics that take place in many towns around the UK each September. Or perhaps you could bake a 'not-going-to-school' cake with your child. You could also take your child to buy a new backpack or lunch box, if their friends are starting school, so that they don't feel as if they are missing out.

If you or your child would like to do something overtly academic, you could buy and start to use a few suitable and interesting workbooks from a large bookshop. Or you could agree on a short period each day when you sit down together to do some reading or writing. Some young children enjoy regular routines, and the feeling of being big enough to do 'schoolwork'. It can help them feel that they are learning too, if they have friends who have just started school. However, unless they ask for something like this, it is not essential. Young children can learn all they need through casual conversation, everyday living, and books that you would read to them anyway.

In the second part of this book, there are brief sections discussing ways to help a young child to read, or to understand simple maths concepts. But please treat these as a last resort. Many children will teach themselves these skills without any direction from parents. Trust your child's innate curiosity, and you are likely to be pleasantly surprised.

De-schooling with an older child

If your child has been to school and you have de-registered them, the situation is a little different. If your child has been bullied, or has struggled with any part of school life, they may be reluctant to do anything educational or 'schoolish' at home. It is important to take time to relax together as a family, to talk about goals and ambitions, and to think about what education means to you.

Rather than worrying about what to do when beginning home education, some families find that it is best to begin with a period of 'de-schooling'. It has been informally established that, the longer a child has been in school, the more time he or she needs to unwind and 'de-school' before beginning any kind of studying or direct learning. A month per year of former schooling is sometimes given as an unofficial guideline. So a child of ten who has been in school for five years may need up to five months before even considering any guided study.

The need for this period of de-schooling varies from child to child, but it is vital not to rush straight into a programme of education. This is particularly the case if your child has left school after a lot of stress. Building family relationships and self-esteem is far more important. You will probably find that, as parents, you will need to de-school too. This includes getting over the idea that learning only happens in a classroom, using workbooks and pens.

If your child asks questions or wants to do something that you see as educational, that's fine. Take his lead as much as you can. It is a good idea to look out for 'teachable moments' when your child shows interest in a specific topic. But do not make it a major issue. If relevant, you can help him to develop the necessary skills to research his own answers. Encourage him to explore a topic in any direction he likes, or to leave it alone when he has had enough.

Moving on from de-schooling

If you or your child are treating home education as a temporary measure, you might want to stay in touch with the National Curriculum for core subjects. The easiest way to do this is to pick up a few workbooks from a large bookshop, and go through them together. You can chat about what you find, or digress to different topics, and can take as long (or short) as you wish. Written work is not necessary, although some children enjoy it.

If you are not expecting to use a school again, there Is no need to use any workbook or curriculum unless these are what your child chooses. 'Education' is a general term, one which will be explored further in the next chapter. Most motivated children will, sooner or later, want to learn for themselves the skills they will need to function as adults. Many home educators consider their style as autonomous: the child takes the lead, the adults facilitate learning as the child wishes.

Alternatively, if your child likes guidance and structure, and if you can afford it, there are schemes of work available from many curriculum providers in the US, and a few in the UK. Space does not permit listing them here, but you can find links online, which should enable you to explore different options.

During your first few months as a home educator, it is a good idea to observe your child's learning style and general interests, to get an idea of what kind of education will work best. Talk with your children, when appropriate, about how and what they would like to learn. If an older child or teenager has ideas about a future career, consider any qualifications they might need, and how they might obtain them. If they have no ideas, you could chat together about what you both consider to be essential in a general education, if anything. Some older children manage to educate themselves effectively by reading books, playing online games, watching documentaries, and asking questions.

Some home educators who start by using structure find themselves gradually veering towards interest-led

How to home educate (in practice)

learning. They explore new topics together, and follow the child's own need to learn at their own rate. Some families use this approach from the beginning, and never emulate a school model at all. Even if it does not seem as if you are covering much educationally, your children will remember and understand vast amounts when they are interested in what they are learning.

At some point you learned how to learn: what questions to ask, how to research and where to find things out for yourself. This probably happened at some point in your secondary school years, or earlier if you were at a good primary school and involved in interesting studies. But you could have learned this at home if you were absorbed in a study of whatever happened to be your passion.

I have heard some adults say that they learned most from being involved in school dramatic productions, or taking part in the orchestra, or a sports team. These were activities they chose for themselves, rather than lessons which they were required to do as part of the school curriculum. Home educated children who are free to follow their own interests are usually eager to learn, and opportunities will arise.

Try to take an objective look at your family. Your situation is not the same as that of any other family in the world. Your children's abilities (and problems) are unique. You may want to ask questions of other home educating families once you have started, but at the beginning the most important thing is to think about your own children's specific needs and interests. Reading about other people's day-to-day home educating lives can let you know that it works, but it can also be discouraging if your children are very different.

If you have avid readers, for instance, there is no point worrying about a reading programme. Just take them to the library and let them loose. If your children write computer programs, you can forget about having to introduce IT skills or computer literacy. They will absorb these things and ask questions as and when they need answers. However, you do not need to worry if, when starting home education, your children cannot read or are not computer literate. They will learn the skills they need when they can do so at their own pace, motivated by their own interests.

As with any childhood milestone, the age range for acquiring educational skills is wide. A ten-year-old home educated child may have no need to read. Perhaps they are learning all they want to know from conversation, from daily life, and from hearing their parents read aloud. By the time they are teenagers they will almost certainly want more independence, and are likely to want to read for themselves. When sufficiently motivated, an older child can usually learn to read in a few weeks without any difficulty.

Does this mean that structured learning is a bad idea? Not at all. Many children choose to follow a course, perhaps taking music lessons, or joining a sports team, or learning a foreign language by a formal method. Teenagers may choose to follow diploma courses or to take exams which will equip them for their chosen careers, or for university entrance. Some decide to go to school or college because they like the set lessons and structure. The important point is that they choose these things for themselves, rather than their being the default whether the children like them or not.

The Education Act in the UK gives a lot of freedom to home educating parents, but it does state that parents must provide an education appropriate to the child's age, ability and aptitude. If by playing, watching TV and general conversation your children are fulfilled and gaining education, there is no problem. But you might need to be concerned if they are frequently bored, or if they appear not to be learning anything. If this happens, it might be a good idea to give a bit of direct input until they gain the maturity to find and follow their own interests.

Home education can be a wonderful adventure, but it will be your personal family adventure. You are undertaking it for your own reasons, for the sake of your unique children. Listen to them, be aware of their needs, and take them seriously. Not only will they then have an education suitable for their own personalities and interests, they will become motivated and eager to learn. Your style will be your own: to suit your preferences and those of your children. There is no need to follow anyone else's philosophy. You need to do what is right for your family, changing and adapting as your children grow up and express new interests.

Our experience

Initially, we thought our sons would go to school in Cyprus after our first year of home education, and that eventually we would return to the UK. So we used some British National Curriculum and other workbooks at first. We planned our days in ways that, we soon discovered, were far too ambitious. Gradually we realised that learning at home was more efficient than in a classroom, and that it was better to follow our sons' motivation and interests rather than planning fixed periods in advance.

In other words, if one of our sons was working on a project that interested him — whether writing a story, or doing some graphic art, or playing a new computer game — then it was best to continue until the activity came to a natural end, rather than to cut into it with the suggestion of something else. Both of them commented, after a couple of years of home education, how much pleasanter it was to work at their own speed, without being regulated by bells and a school timetable.

What suited our family best was a mixture of parent-initiated education, child-led learning, educational books and web-sites, plus music and art lessons with outside teachers. Our style evolved as the boys grew and matured. They developed more specific interests as they started thinking about possible future careers. We started using a structured academic course, at their choosing, after a couple of years, but it was only a small part of their general and eclectic education. We often took a detour from the coursework when my sons asked questions about things — which covered random topics such as Newton's laws or the politics of Kosovo.

We discovered that there was no limit to what they could understand, if they wanted to know something and were prepared to find out. This is a major advantage of home education. Instead of being limited by fixed periods and required to follow a specific curriculum, there is time for much deeper study of topics that catch children's interest.

Inevitably we had some bad days with frustrations, complaints, boredom or general irritation. I tried to listen and to find out what had caused a problem. Then either I encouraged the boys to find their own solutions, or suggested we do something different. No two days were ever the same, and frustrations and squabbles are part of family life. Conflict resolution can be educational in itself if you are prepared to take the time to help your children see each other's points of view and to find a mutually satisfactory solution to whatever issues arise.

I see education as a process of opening doors. My

children discovered many of these doors by themselves, and I could show them the existence of others, with a peep of what lay beyond. They liked me to read aloud to them for at least half an hour so each day, even when they were teenagers. So I chose books, sometimes classics, that I wanted to introduce them to. Some were books which they would probably not have chosen for themselves. Not everyone will want to do this; some children do not like parents to read aloud once they can read for themselves. But I offer it as an example. It was an enjoyable way for me to share my love of literature with my sons.

CHAPTER FOUR
What is education?

What is education?

Something strange happened in the 20th century. 'Education' became equated with 'schooling'. There are people who think this is a conspiracy to get children conforming to governmental standards, and there may be some truth in this. School curriculums change regularly, and the agenda includes training young people for citizenship and employment.

Nonetheless, most of us went through the school system, and probably learned a fair amount even if we have forgotten the majority. But we also learned a great deal outside school at other structured or unstructured activities. Perhaps you took music lessons or belonged to a Scouting or religious group. Perhaps, like I did, you read dozens of books in the school holidays. Yet in our Western countries, despite free speech and the ability to ask questions, there are still many people who think that someone who does not go to school cannot be educated.

When you begin home educating, it is a good idea to spend some time considering what education means to you. What should you be concerned about as you embark on home education?

Here are the first two of definitions of the word 'education' from an online dictionary:

The act or process of imparting or acquiring general knowledge, developing the powers of reasoning and judgment, and generally of preparing oneself or others intellectually for mature life.

The act or process of imparting or acquiring particular knowledge or skills, as for a profession

So when people undertake to educate their children in compliance with the law, they should primarily be giving them an overview of 'general knowledge'. They should also help their children and teenagers to weigh up what they see and to use their reason, in preparation for adult life. In addition, parents need to enable their children to learn whatever specifics they need for their interests, and for their future careers.

As stated before, in the UK there are no specific rules about what home educated children have to study. They do not have to do any maths, or know anything about history or geography or science. Every family is free to decide what constitutes education suitable for each child.

Does that make you feel uncomfortable? If so, is that because of your own educational background? Or is it because you feel that it is inherently important for children to have an understanding of the wider world, and how things work?

Consider, for a moment, the reverse point of view. Children in secondary schools study a wide range of subjects. But is it necessary that everybody understand — for instance — how two chemicals will react together? As another example, will it affect their adult life negatively if they do not know what products are grown in the different South American countries? Or will it be a major problem if someone never understands the basic trigonometric theorems?

And perhaps the most important questions of all: how many of these and other things which you studied at school do you still recall? How many have you needed to use since leaving school?

Of course, general knowledge, as suggested by the first definition of education given above, will probably include some of these things. If you travel at all, your children are likely to develop an understanding of maps, and features of the landscape. Most children ask questions about any topic that occurs to them. When they meet and interact with people from different cultures, they will learn something about what those differences mean. As you bake, or measure a room for wallpaper, or share a packet of biscuits, they will grasp simple arithmetical concepts.

These are all part of everyday family life; home educated children are not isolated from the world. They can learn a great deal through discussion, through understanding age-appropriate news stories from the television or Internet, from reading or sharing historical or other fiction. But whereas children at school sometimes lose the motivation to keep asking questions and discovering new things, those educated at home tend to keep it. As a parent you do not need to know all the answers; the Internet is an excellent resource for almost any topic that arises. In looking up information about any subject online, you are demonstrating simple research skills.

As for particular knowledge, that will depend almost entirely on your child. If they are going to be chemical pathologist, they need to know a great deal of chemistry. But if that is their passion, they will choose to learn as much as they can. The study of chemistry is no more (or less) important than, for instance, the study of music. A gifted musician will spend a lot of time learning theory and practising pieces. Yet we don't require every child to learn complex music theory, or even to start to play the piano. Nor should we require every child to study chemistry, unless that is something that interests them.

School at home

Some parents who decide to take their children out of school continue thinking that the schooling model is basically correct. Home educators do not have large classrooms or the limitations of a timetable, yet there are families who continue with other schooling practices. Perhaps the children study subjects at fixed times, or use exercise books to answer text book questions. Some children apparently walk out of their front door with a backpack on and walk in at the back door for 'homeschool'. They have fixed periods of study, raising their hands to ask questions during their set educational hours.

While this is not my style, there is nothing wrong with this system, if it suits your child. If they hope to go back to school eventually, it might be a good idea to keep some school-type traditions. But you have to be quite disciplined to follow this model, and even if the parents like it, some children do not. If you are going to follow this model, then you can plan your own curriculum, if you have the time, expertise and enthusiasm to do so.

Alternatively, if finances permit, you can use a ready-made system. The US has many curricula that can be

What is education?

taught at home; most are affiliated to a religious group. The UK does not tend to produce this kind of curriculum, but there are many places offering online teaching or tutoring. With these, you can pick and choose subjects, and have them monitored by trained teachers.

If you decide to use a ready-made curriculum, or one of the distance learning possibilities, find out as much as you can about the various options. Check their web sites for the philosophy and pricing, and how to order materials. Before making any decision, it is a good idea to talk to other families who have used these curricula, if possible, and read a range of reviews.

Take note, too, of your children's interests and learning styles. A child who learns through his hands, for instance, is unlikely to be inspired by a curriculum with a lot of reading and writing. A child who is advanced in some areas and slower in others will not want to be limited by a curriculum that has rigid 'grade level' expectations.

A good educational provider will have contact details and should be willing to answer questions. They may also direct you to a related online group or forum. They might be willing to send out samples, or offer a trial period. It is important to take the time to look at the style of material, and discuss with your children whether the courses look inspiring and interesting. What appeals to one will not necessarily appeal to another.

Autonomous education

At the other end of the home education spectrum, there are a number of autonomous educators. This is similar to American 'unschooling', where children learn whatever they want to, in their own way. Intrinsic motivation is what guides them, in the same way as it directs toddlers to explore and ask questions. Parents give input only when asked, and the children are free to do anything they feel like.

Some children benefit from this kind of child-led learning. Perhaps this is more so when they have never been to school and have not lost the questioning, eager enthusiasm of the toddler years. But even amongst those, there are some children who are far more eager to learn than others. Personalities are different, motivations are different.

Because autonomous learning is so effective when it works, it can be easy — when reading about families who follow this philosophy — to assume that it is the best way of educating at home. That can cause concern if children do not ask any questions, are not intrinsically motivated and do not seem to be learning by osmosis.

But some children's personalities tend towards the path of least resistance. If given no direction at all, these children will gravitate towards spending all day watching television, or reading the same books, or playing computer games. There is nothing wrong with these activities when the child is in control. But they can too easily become compulsive, sapping their energy, leaving them with little interest in anything else. A child's brain is not the same as an adult one, and it can be very hard for a child or teenager, involved in something compulsive, to take a step away and do something else.

Eclectic home education

Probably the majority of British home educators fall somewhere between these two extremes. Many are keen to follow their children's interests, but still see it as important to teach basic maths or science. Some may opt for formal courses, particularly with teenagers who

What is education?

might want to go to university to study academic topics. Some pick and choose one or two appealing text books from bookshops, while mostly following their children's leading.

Others might encourage self-directed learning but put aside a short period each day to read aloud — historical fiction, perhaps — or to work on maths problems with each child individually. Some might plan days out to places of interest, or have set times for computer use with boundaries as to what the children can do.

There is no one method of home education which works well for every child. So listen to your children's needs and wishes, but also to your own convictions. You, as a parent, are the person responsible for providing education, and you need to feel confident and comfortable about it. You do not have to justify your methods or decisions, but it is useful to be able to explain them to others who are curious.

If you try one style but are not happy with it, or if you sense that the children are not learning or enjoying life, then try something else. If what you are doing seems to be working well, stay with it. There is no need to compare yourself with your friends, or with anyone else. It can be hard to stand back and observe, and it may take months, even years to get the right balance. What works well for one child may be a disaster for a younger sibling.

Remember that no decision about home education has to be forever.

Our experience

I assumed, at first, that school-at-home was the way to go. We started by trying to follow UK National Curriculum guidelines and using relevant text books, with an approximate timetable. It was too stressful for us all.

We adjusted it. We adapted it. We tried studying different things, and put aside some text books that did not inspire the boys. We took days off for visitors. We made new plans. We experimented with the autonomous method, and it worked well for our older son, but our younger son wanted some structure.

We started thinking about university and the difficulty of taking relevant exams when not living in the UK. Eventually — after much research — we decided, as a family, to use an American curriculum for the teenage years. However, we saw it just one part of their education, and the boys continued learning a great deal through books, discussion, computer games and also from friends and groups they joined. We called ourselves eclectic educators, working mostly autonomously around a curriculum.

It worked, on the whole, for us. That does not necessarily mean it would work for anyone else. Each home educating family needs to find their own path, and adjust to the unique needs of each child within the family.

Educational basics

In the middle of the 20th century, people talked about the 'three Rs' of education. This is a tad ironic in that only one of the three actually begins with the letter R. Reading, writing and arithmetic were seen as the core to all learning. They were the skills in which children were educated (and sometimes drilled) until they were proficient.

Reading, in my view, still ranks as an essential skill. Audio books and the ability to have documents read aloud by apps are useful for cars. They are wonderful tools for people who are blind, or who have specific learning problems meaning that they are unable to read. But for the majority of us, reading and literacy are still crucial. For all the dire predictions of twenty years ago, real books are still bought, whether in print or electronic form. Magazines and newspapers continue to be produced too.

However, handwriting has mostly been replaced by typing on computers or phones. People might handwrite shopping lists or journals; but those are choices rather than necessities. I would suggest that general computer literacy and research skills are far more important than handwriting for the modern child.

As for arithmetic: understanding how numbers work is essential for many fields. But the technological revolution has changed our needs and practices. Knowing how to do long multiplication or division on paper is less important when phones have calculators, and we can ask Google to do complex arithmetic.

Rather than drilling our children with rapid mental arithmetic skills, it is far more important, in my view, to give them an understanding of mathematical concepts. This will enable them to use calculators intelligently. The ability to reason and work things out from first principles is more important than knowing arithmetic 'facts'.

So, a little tongue-in-cheek, I consider that the postmodern or 21st century 'three Rs' could be listed as: reading, research and reasoning.

The more you read aloud to your children as babies and toddlers, the more they are likely to be interested in books and the process of reading. Scientists regularly discover more benefits of reading aloud to small children. Advanced language skills and greater understanding of other people are just a couple of them. Children familiar with enjoyable books are more likely to want to read for themselves, too.

However, each child learns to read in a different way. If you are home educating there is no pressure to teach them to read as early as possible. The majority of children, if given plenty of books and opportunity, acquire the skill to read fluently, sooner or later. This typically happens between the ages of about three and ten, with the peak probably around ages six to eight.

If your children read widely, they are likely to learn a large amount with little effort. You can encourage them to read non-fiction as well as fiction, although not every child appreciates non-fiction. This is not a problem; a great deal can be learned from historical fiction, or novels set in other countries. Fiction in general is excellent in helping children understand other people and to develop empathy.

If your children do not like reading (or even if they do), you can still read aloud to them. This is a wonderful way of drawing families closer and introducing your own childhood favourites. You can read books they would not choose for themselves, which can spark new interests or inspire them to follow different authors.

If your children mainly like non-fiction, there are excellent books available on almost any topic. If you browse your library or local bookshop, you should find a wide range of non-fiction 'educational' books, appropriate for a range of ages. Some are written with humour. Many have helpful diagrams and images, to suit almost any interest or topic.

Until recently, sociologists recommended that under the age of about five, children should not be exposed to computers, tablets, or even television. Anything on a screen, they said, can delay development. More recent

What is education?

research suggests that this is not as much of a problem as had been thought; however it is self-evident that too much time in front of a screen can also lead to lack of interaction with other people, and also too little free play and exercise.

It is worth reading the latest research on this, but as with most child-related issues, it is best to find some balance. It is unlikely that any harm will come from regular Skype calls with grandparents, for instance. Short children's TV shows now and again, can distract a grumpy child. An age-appropriate film, shared with a parent, can be a good way to spend a rainy afternoon with a lively toddler.

After the age of about four or five, limited screen exposure is generally considered a good thing, again in moderation. There are some excellent educational computer games and apps as well as some great TV shows and films intended for young children. Do exercise judgement: if a game or film is rated 12 or 15, there is likely to be content in it which could be disturbing to a younger child.

Remember, too, that young children mostly learn through play, either alone or with others. They need physical objects — such as building blocks or cars or small figurines — to help their motor skills develop. They also need to be active, running around in fresh air, or at least moving around the house.

Still, it is important that children become familiar with technology, and develop some computer literacy. Once your child starts to use a computer or tablet, basic skills are likely to be learned intuitively. Young children seem to find technology much easier to master than adults do. There is no need for special child-oriented software. You probably have a drawing or photo-manipulation program on your computer already, or can find a free one to download. Playing with images is an excellent way to start understanding menus and shortcuts, as well as touch-screens, and to begin to see what can be done on computers.

Children as young as five or six can use ordinary word processors to type letters and stories. Younger ones can dictate, if they want to. They will quickly develop keyboard familiarity if you encourage them. Children who struggle with the manual dexterity of writing with a pencil can more easily become confident in typing. There are many applications that teach touch-typing, and it can be started at almost any age.

For older children, I used to recommend computer games as an excellent educational resource. A great deal of history, geography and politics could be learned from some of these. Unfortunately, some of the recent games have become more graphically violent and less educational. If you include computer games in your household, it is important to watch out for signs of a computer world becoming more real to a child than family life, and to take appropriate action to limit their use if necessary.

Most research is much easier to do on the Internet than in books. Not that I wish to discourage dictionaries, encyclopaedias or atlases. We regularly used to have one or other of these at the table during the course of a meal when questions arose that we could not answer ourselves. But reference books are expensive and become out of date quickly. It is a constructive use of computers and phones to be able to find answers to questions quickly, or to browse articles related to a topic without having to page through heavy volumes.

Education used to involve a lot of fact-learning: of rote knowledge about geography, for instance, or

What is education?

historical dates, or scientific theories. But scientific and technological knowledge has now become greater than any individual can understand or remember. Thus one of the most useful skills we can impart to our children is knowing where to look online for information or articles. We need to help them understand how to filter the helpful pages from the unhelpful, and how to apply what we read to life and learning.

Home education does not have to be anything like classroom teaching. Instead, you can adapt your days depending on your family's interests and on what is available locally. The first few months of home education can be a wonderful opportunity for getting to know your neighbourhood better. Perhaps you could spend time at the library and any museums or other nearby places of interest.

If your children ask for some sort of structure, try to plan a specific activity for each day to give a focus. For instance, you could begin each morning with reading aloud, or playing a family board game. If this does not seem to be sufficient, try brainstorming together with your children. Together you should be able to come up with a rough timetable that covers the mornings. Try choosing some interesting work books or text books from a local or online bookshop. Then make sure that your timetable is flexible, something to fall back on when nothing else happens, rather than an unchangeable plan for every day.

Books and articles about home education can be inspiring and helpful. But they tend to focus on the successes, and gloss somewhat over the problems. It is encouraging to know that home educated children usually grow up to get good jobs and to have fulfilled lives. But how many bad days did they have? How much parental input or guidance was there alongside the child-led learning? How many days dragged along with the children fighting, or even wishing they could go to school?

If you are feeling discouraged, try doing something different. Pack a picnic and spend the day at a nearby beach or park. Or invite some other home educating families over and make pizza together. Or, if your children are happily occupied, create a blog and write about your day as honestly as you can. If you are brave enough to share it publicly, you may find that your horrible day is a tremendous encouragement to other struggling home educators.

Our experience

Since we did not start home educating until our sons were eleven and nine, they could already read fluently. They were also used to both typing and hand-writing. They had plenty of interests and were highly computer literate, although that mainly due to the computers we had at home, related to my husband's work.

So, once we moved beyond the compulsion to keep up with the National Curriculum, most of their education was based on what they felt inspired to do at the time. At various points during the next few years one or both of the boys became involved in: web-page design; writing short stories and starting to write novels; stamp collecting; programming; graphic design; art of various sorts; music — both self-taught and from outside teachers.

In addition, they learned a surprising amount of history and geography from civilisation-building computer games. They spent a lot of time playing with Lego, Meccano and K'nex, which are all excellent tools for developing maths and technology skills. Occasionally they would draw scale plans of their bedrooms, which involved measuring, accurate drawing, and scaling down. My younger son was keen on cooking and baking, too. He did not like arithmetic on paper, but when doubling (or halving) recipes, multiplication and division are used in practical ways, along with concepts such as measuring and weighing of ingredients.

Learning styles

We all learn differently. This is self-evident when we look at babies and toddlers: some are eager to explore the world; others prefer to sit and observe. Some learn to crawl before they are six months old; some are nearer nine or ten months old. Some never crawl and shuffle around on their bottoms instead. Speech development is even more varied. I knew a child who could speak and understand about a hundred clear words at just a year old. I knew another who had only about five distinct words when he was two. Yet by the time they were about five, there was little difference in their language abilities.

Many years ago the Reception class teacher in my sons' UK school told me that in all her years of teaching she had never come across two children who learned to read in exactly the same way. She adjusted her style, and the books used, to suit each individual child within her class. She was an exceptionally talented teacher, who relied on the help of volunteer parents as well as her classroom assistant. This variation in learning styles can be another positive reason for home education, where each child's needs can be taken into account much more easily.

There are various ways of classifying learning styles. The best known and simplest is that which divides the population into three groups: visual learners, auditory learners, and kinaesthetic learners. My personal experience is that a fourth style is also prevalent: that of verbal (or linguistic) learning. We can all use all the styles at times, but for each individual person, one or two are likely to stand out as the strongest.

High visual learners tend to need diagrams or pictures to learn and remember things. They understand speaking better if they can also observe body language. They may find graphical internet sites or videos to be a good way to learn rapidly., and they prefer maps to spoken or written directions. Many people with good visual learning are artistically inclined, although learning style and abilities are not necessarily linked.

High auditory learners are more attuned to the sense of hearing. They tend to learn well from talks, or audio recordings, and remember better the things they have heard rather than those they have seen. They need verbal explanations in preference to diagrams or maps. Many who learn best by auditory learning are musically inclined, but, again, this is not always the case.

High kinaesthetic learners are those who learn best by doing something. They require a hands-on approach to anything new and will gain much more from carrying out an activity than they would by reading about it or watching someone else do it. When they must read or listen to something, they need to be physically active in some way, if only swinging their legs or tapping their chairs. High kinaesthetic learning can lead someone to be good at sports or other physical activities.

High verbal learners are those who learn best through words — usually written or printed ones. They will understand printed instructions better than spoken ones or maps, and will prefer to read a book or textual web page rather than to watch a video if they want to understand something. Those who are primarily verbal learners tend to be early readers, and may be good at

What is education?

writing (though, again, not necessarily)

If your image of education is of children sitting at desks and absorbing facts from lectures or books, you may struggle to educate a child whose strongest learning styles are not auditory or verbal. You might think your children are being annoying if they will not stop fidgeting, or seem uninterested in reading. You might feel in despair if your first child completed workbooks easily and confidently, whereas your second child moans, groans, and then takes two hours to complete one page.

On the other hand, you might be a high kinaesthetic learner, who prefers an active, hands-on education, with field trips and practical science and craft activities. If your child prefers to curl up on a sofa reading a book, you might feel bewildered, wondering how to encourage more action.

Understanding learning styles will help you see that apparent problems of this kind are easily solved by adjusting your home education practice to suit your children's learning styles. Talking, reading and hands-on activities are all important: but a primarily kinaesthetic child may need to run around the garden every few minutes, or get up to punch a pillow while you are talking. A child with high visual learning may need to doodle while listening, or read books with plenty of diagrams, whereas a high verbal child may find diagrams distracting.

As home educators, it is most effective, and also most pleasant for all involved, if we are aware of the way our children learn best. Remember that UK education law states that parents must cause their children to be educated according to their age, aptitude and ability, and any special needs. If your child needs to cartwheel around the room in order to learn anything, it is unlikely that a school would provide such an opportunity. Home educators can tune in to their children's needs and styles, and help them have a truly personalised education.

Another theory that I find helpful is that of multiple intelligences. 'Intelligence' is a rather over-used and misunderstood word in some circles. People tend to use it to imply excellence at certain academic subjects (particularly sciences, maths and English), or perhaps when referring to the kind of person who can do well in IQ tests.

Yet we probably all know of people whom we consider to be highly intelligent, yet they are terrible at any kind of number-work and score badly on IQ tests. Equally we may know of academic people, brilliant at maths or sciences, who seem to lack any common sense or the ability to communicate effectively. It seems self-evident to me that there are many kinds of intelligence. Nearly everybody excels at something.

So I find this theory helpful. Experts have isolated seven main strands of intelligence: inter-personal, intra-personal, kinaesthetic, musical, logical/mathematical, verbal/linguistic, and visual/spatial. The last three of these tend to be measured on IQ tests, but for maturity and day-to-day living, the first four are just as important.

A person with high social/inter-personal intelligence tends to require discussion and group learning. They may be an Extravert, needing other people around to feel energised. Or they may need other people for bouncing ideas. In contrast, someone with high solitary/intra-personal intelligence is more likely to be an Introvert. People excelling in this need time to themselves to reflect, and may learn best when they are away from other people.

Someone with high physical/kinaesthetic intelligence

What is education?

tends to need constant action. They may need to take part in sports or other physical activities such as gardening or juggling. Someone with high aural/musical intelligence probably has a good sense of rhythm and pitch. They will benefit more than most from learning a musical instrument or dancing, particularly if they also have high kinaesthetic intelligence.

Someone with high logical/mathematical intelligence is naturally good with reasoning, likely to grasp new concepts easily, and to think clearly. Someone with high verbal/linguistic intelligence will probably be confident with both spoken and written language. They may enjoy communicating and playing with words. Someone with high visual/spatial intelligence is likely to have a good sense of direction. They will be happiest working with artwork, images, diagrams or other visual media.

Most people have some skill related to several of these intelligences, and can develop abilities in others if motivated and encouraged. Unlike learning styles, which describe how we best learn, multiple intelligences look at what we are able to do. Skills which do not come naturally can often be learned.

It is vitally important to respect our children's needs. Sometimes these are obvious, but not always. So understanding their intelligences in this context can be helpful. For instance, if you have children who like music from a young age — perhaps listening to music to go to sleep, or moving around rhythmically to music — they may want to bang saucepans as toddlers and learn to sing or play an instrument as they grow older.

However, if you have a child with low musical intelligence, they may have no desire to learn to play an instrument or sing. That does not mean that you should avoid playing music at home if you like doing so; when children are little you can try singing or dancing with them too. But be aware of their feelings, and avoid trying to persuade them to join in if they are not willing, or find it embarrassing.

Children with kinaesthetic intelligence will need some kind of active outlet, which will partly depend on their other intelligences. If they also have musical intelligence, they might like to take up dancing, or learn to play the drums. However if rather than musical intelligence they have high inter-personal intelligence, they might be happiest playing in team sports at a leisure centre. A child high in solitary intelligence as well as kinaesthetic might prefer an outlet to their active nature in gardening or swimming.

Traditional education usually encourages verbal and mathematical skills. A child high in these may benefit from a curriculum. If you prefer not to use one, you may need to provide more books, puzzles and games than you would to a child who is not so strong in these areas. But if these are not your children's primary intelligences, it is vital that they are not made to feel inferior to more academically inclined children.

The theory of autonomous education says that children learn all they need to learn, when they are ready to do so, in their own way. Their choices are likely to reflect their main intelligences. As they practise, so they develop in skill.

Some parents believe that their children need a balanced education, and a variety of skills. They may worry that their children will lack skills they need as adults if they are left to their own choices all the time. I used to worry a little when I read about prodigies like Mozart. His musical skills were at genius level, but he

What is education?

had little chance to develop any others. He ended up depressed and in debt, dying young.

Naturally we hope that our children will grow into well-rounded adults. But this does not mean that we should attempt to teach them to use all the intelligences equally. To take extreme examples, nobody would force a tone-deaf child to take singing lessons, or expect a blind child to study visual art. All children have strengths and weaknesses, and there are some topics and intelligences which may be inappropriate for them.

On the other hand, a tone-deaf child might have an excellent sense of rhythm, and a blind child might make a brilliant sculptor. A quiet child with high solitary intelligence may never develop strong social intelligence, but may enjoy writing emails to relatives or taking part in online forums where he can be anonymous. Trying to make him socialise may push him more into his solitary state; but he can still learn social skills in his own way, in his own time.

Home education can be enriching and rewarding for both parents and children, and a positive learning experience for all. But don't try to make your children fit into your own preconceived ideas of what they should learn, or to follow your own intelligences if theirs are different. Listen to them, learn with them, and encourage them to explore and develop skills as and when they are appropriate.

Our experience

One of my sons has high visual intelligence. One day, when he was around thirteen and working on some computer graphics, he came across a paragraph in a computer arts magazine about using sines and cosines. He asked me what they were.

We happened to have a GCSE maths book that covered basic trigonometry, and fortunately I remembered at least the gist of the topic from my own secondary school days. I was able to teach him in about half an hour what would have taken at least a term in school. A few weeks later he was using these functions confidently in his art, at a level far beyond what I had explained, because he was motivated to do so.

He never did learn the algebraic theories that go alongside trigonometry, but was able to work out those which he needed. Mathematics and logic were a sideline to his visual intelligence.

CHAPTER FIVE
What about Socialising?

Socialising in theory

It is not difficult to see that, academically, home education can be more effective than classroom teaching, if only because children have the chance to learn at their own rate, with one-to-one attention. Research shows that many home educated children achieve academic goals easily, and are able to think for themselves, learning anything they want to know with confidence.

But doubts are often expressed about socialising, or 'socialisation'. It is often one of the first questions new home educators are asked, hence it is worth thinking about right at the beginning. Are home educated children isolated from other children? Are they able to make friends with a wide variety of people? Will they be able to fit into society as adults if they have not been through the ups and downs of school life? Do they become too dependent on their parents? Are they reluctant to go out to meet new situations and people?

Being sociable

People, on the whole, are social creatures. Being sociable, at least to some extent, is part of our nature. It is true that some folk like to be with others for significant amounts of the time, while others prefer just one or two friends and need frequent time to themselves. But we all need other people for companionship. If we enable children to develop in their own ways, they will usually relate first to family members and then to other people, when they are ready to do so.

Clearly children need to meet people in order to be sociable, but home educators do not tend to be isolated from the community. Some children naturally make friends with everyone they meet; some do not. Parents, who know their children well, can introduce a shy child to other people at relaxed times, in safe environments. This is much healthier than pushing them into situations where they may become withdrawn or upset.

Social skills

Social skills include – for instance – culturally appropriate manners, knowing how to greet different people, and joining in conversations without interrupting. They are the ways we learn to relate to others in order to build relationships, to be able to communicate effectively, and to spend time enjoying company. Children primarily learn their social skills and cultural expectations from their parents. So the most important thing you can do is to model the kind of behaviour you would like to see.

Social skills can be helpful in putting other people at ease. While some skills – such as saying 'thank you' – are widely expected, others will vary from family to family, even within the same culture group. It is important to be able to adapt, when necessary, to make other people feel comfortable. It is vital, therefore, particularly if you are going to travel, that you explain to your children that how your family behaves is something you have chosen, not a moral issue.

There are few absolute rules about social skills, as they vary so much across different cultures. In some it is appropriate to eat with fingers, for instance; in others you may be required to eat with chopsticks, or with knives and forks. You may expect your children to use cutlery because it is generally appropriate in the places you visit. But it is not rude or uncivilised to eat in different ways in other settings, if that is culturally appropriate.

Home educated children are likely to meet a wide variety of people. They may find it interesting to see how, even within one neighbourhood, there are many different ways of behaving. If you are comfortable with your own social skills, it is easier to discuss those of other cultures, and to adapt when appropriate.

Socialisation

The word 'socialisation' implies something more than merely being sociable and acquiring appropriate social skills. One dictionary defines socialisation as: 'the modification from infancy of an individual's behaviour to conform with the demands of social life.'

Rather than expecting children to learn through imitation and gentle reminders, 'socialisation' implies deliberate behaviour modification. While parents may sometimes attempt this (for instance, by regularly asking a child to stop interrupting when friends are visiting) it is done in an atmosphere of love, alongside explanations. There should also be a model of the expected behaviour by the parents.

Sending a child to school, however good and friendly it might be, to learn to have his behaviour modified is a rather chilling thought. It suggests firstly that parents have little influence, and secondly that all children should behave in the same way, all the time. The idea, moreover, of expecting our children to conform to the demands of social life suggests that they should be made to suppress their natural desires — and even beliefs — in order to fit in with the majority.

In my view, it is better to raise children who understand the reasons for social expectations and skills, and who are able to query things they disagree with. Mature children can easily understand the difference between moral or ethical issues, and those which are merely social or cultural. It is right to stand firm on important moral principles, but as far as social or cultural things go, it is fine to be willing to adapt to those around us. Making a deliberate choice to adapt is not the same as being required to observe rigid conformity.

Peer pressure

Peer pressure is a well-known problem of the pre-teen and teenage years, and encapsulates the negative side of enforced socialising. When children go through periods of insecurity, or want to be part of the 'in-crowd', they sometimes adopt dangerous habits in order to prove that they are 'cool', or that they are not pandering to their parents. This is why so many teenagers turn to drugs, alcohol, smoking or promiscuity — not for any true satisfaction, but in the hope of being popular.

It should be obvious that this does not work. It is observable that those who stand apart from peer pressure are more likely to be respected by those who are more mature. Sadly too many teens, emotional already due to hormonal instabilities, fall into the trap of wanting to be popular. When that happens, peer socialising can become an extremely negative influence.

If your child is displaying negative peer-pressure related traits, you might want to read the book 'How to really love your teenager' by Ross Campbell. This book helps parents to express their unconditional love to teens in ways that are heard and understood. It also gives suggestions for dealing with some of the problems which can occur during the teenage years.

It is rare for long-term home educated children to experiment seriously with dangerous behaviour, or to worry about whether or not they can be accepted by their peers. But it can happen; teens of some personality types are more prone to this than others, and some youth groups or other teenage gatherings can be just as cliquey as those in a classroom.

Still, home educated children generally make friends of all ages rather than just those of similar age. Deep down they know that they do not need to compete, or to pretend to be someone different, in order to be accepted for who they are. Free from having to spend several hours per day with the same people of the same age, home educated teenagers more naturally treat everyone else as individuals, irrelevant of looks, style, or inclinations.

Our experience

Our two sons were brought up in similar ways, with the same parents, but clearly had different temperaments from birth. One of them, as a toddler, was quiet and observant, waiting in the sidelines before joining in any new activity. The other was outgoing and friendly, eager to join in anything new. When they came home from school, one needed time to himself to unwind after what seemed to him to be a tiring day of being with people.

The other needed someone to play with, after what he thought of as a quiet day where he could not do much socialising.

My role was not to try to change either of them, but to encourage them to be themselves. As I look back, I am thankful that both were educated at home during the potentially difficult teenage years. They were able to develop as individuals without having to please teachers or other students. Living abroad, we learned a lot about cultural expectations, and what might be considered rude or unfriendly in other countries, and we could talk about social situations as they occurred.

Socialising in practice

The theory is all very well, but in practice every child is different. If you have several children, or if your child regularly plays with cousins or neighbouring children, then you can probably ignore this chapter. However, if you have an only child, it may be more difficult to create social situations. Moreover, some children are naturally shy, and find it difficult to mix or talk to others.

So here are a few suggestions, if you are worried about how to help your home educated children to become well-rounded and sociable.

Toddlers

When you watch small children, it is apparent that sociability and friendliness are first of all a product of the child's innate personality. One toddler may be shy and clingy, yet his brother, raised in the same way, might be outgoing and eager to meet new people. There is a popular viewpoint suggesting that children should be thrown into the company of others in environments such as nursery school as early as possible. The idea is that this way they will learn to get along with others and to do without the parents.

However, toddlers who are not naturally sociable are likely to feel their shyness reinforced by such a group. It may cause them to become even less likely to join in the next time. They may eventually adjust, because they have no choice. But trying to force clingy children to be sociable before they are ready is not helpful.

It is far better, for such children, to introduce them to others one at a time in their own homes. When they are ready, you might join an informal mother-and-toddler group where you can stay to give the child added security and supervision. This enables them to explore their new environment knowing you are there, and to learn to play alongside others at their own pace.

Young children

If you watch any group of young children together, some will be obvious leaders, some will try to make friends with each other at once, and others will wait on the sidelines or become upset. Those who are already sociable will not become more so by being in a group, although they will probably enjoy it. Some children, by the age of four or five, may be eager to get into a classroom, to find new resources, more children, and different adults to give them fresh ideas. For such a child, the early years in a good school may be an exciting adventure where they make lots of friends.

Indeed, highly sociable children might find home education somewhat lonely at times if they do not have brothers or sisters, or if there are no other children to play with locally. When looking at what is best for your child, it is important to consider their personality and preferences socially, as well as academically. If you decide that your local school would provide a good environment for your sociable child, it does not necessarily rule out home education at some point in the future.

Other children growing beyond toddlerhood remain shy, uncertain of themselves, sometimes not yet able to communicate clearly with strangers. Such a child would not be helped by having to spend time in a classroom where many of the other children are likely to be talkative and outgoing. Children with this temperament might become labelled as 'slow', and may begin to see themselves as misfits even at this age.

Shy children often find it easier to relate to adults than to other children at first, particularly if they think deeply or are less energetic than others their age. This is not a problem if you are home educating. If your children do not have grandparents nearby, perhaps an elderly neighbour might appreciate spending time with them. You might know someone in hospital whom you could visit. If you take your children regularly to parks or groups related to their interests, they will come across children of all ages. Unless these other children are actively unfriendly, your children are likely to begin to want to relate to them so long as they are not pressurised to do so.

Older children and teenagers

As home educated children grow up, they will probably get to know those around them — librarians, neighbours, other people they meet. They will observe the way you relate to others, and are likely to imitate the way you react. Even if shy and clingy in the early years, most children, if not pushed to make friends, will gradually become more outgoing. Most children are able to carry on a conversation with others as they grow up and become more confident. Indeed, a shyer, observant child is more likely to notice appropriate social skills in others and to imitate them. A lively and extraverted child who never stops to think before speaking may sometimes offend people unintentionally.

You may find that your children want to join group activities based on their interests. Sports, music and dancing are popular, and provide peer groups in friendly settings with shared goals and interests. If you belong to a church or other religious group, there will probably be activities that your children will join in with naturally, along with others of similar age.

If none of those is relevant, you might want to consider Scouting groups or similar organisations. In addition, you may have a local home education support group, who might meet for craft activities, or visit places of interest together. With any group, success depends very much on the leaders. So be sure that you and your child feel comfortable with anything they try out before making a commitment.

Make sure, too, that you consider each child's individual needs. A quiet child who enjoys being alone may be perfectly happy with just one or two friends, and might only rarely want to participate in group activities.

Dealing with bullies

I have heard people claim that children need to go to school in order to learn to deal with bullies. This makes no sense to me. Some children who are bullied becomes bullies themselves. Others withdraw, or become depressed, or remain passive victims. It generally takes adult intervention to sort out the problem: it is not something that children learn to deal with by themselves.

Besides, even for those who turn around and fight, bullying does not teach appropriate or useful ways of relating to others. As adults we are unlikely to have our books torn, or our hair pulled; nor can we turn around and punch people who offend us. It is more useful to meet a mixture of people in real life, as happens in a home educating environment. As we do so, we learn that we do not necessarily get along with everyone; but that there are usually amicable ways of sorting out differences.

If you raise your children to ask questions, to think for themselves, and to know that they are valued and likeable, they are less likely to give in to those who might try to intimidate them when they are older. Different kinds of bullying sometimes happen in adult life: sexism, racism, belittling and other problems can occur in workplaces, and even sometimes on public transport or in shops. But if we teach our children to stand up for what they believe and to understand that everyone is different, we are taking a small step towards a more peaceable society.

Our experience

When we moved to Cyprus, our first few months were taken up with new experiences, getting to know new colleagues and their families, and finding our feet in a different culture.

My younger son was lonely at times, sometimes missing day-to-day school life. We found a local Cub Scouts which he attended for a year, and he joined a Greek-speaking choir. We made the effort to spend more time with our colleagues' children, and towards the end of our first academic year, we discovered an island-wide group of home educators who met monthly.

Local children and teenagers were not particularly friendly. They did not have much time to themselves anyway, with school hours from approximately 7.30am

What about socialising?

to 1.30pm, and usually at least two or three hours of homework each afternoon. But they were not aggressive. They simply lacked interest in foreigners like ourselves.

Once our sons hit the teenage years, they developed more friendships with people in the youth group. Almost everybody there had lived in more than one country; many had dual nationality. We went to a church where there were over thirty different nationalities represented. Both our sons joined the church music group, and there were various other local events which gave us a reasonably active social life. We learned to observe how other people behaved, not to copy them or even to attempt to fit in, but to be able to communicate with them effectively.

We had a steady stream of visitors from the UK, too. It was great to be able to go out for days or spend time with our guests rather than having to worry about school term dates or early bedtimes.

CHAPTER SIX
Parenting while Home Educating

Parenting theories

As a home educator, I had plenty of time to think through my philosophy of parenting, which inevitably affected our educational style. I offer this chapter for those wondering which kinds of parents are most suited to educating their children at home, and what parenting style is most effective. Not that I have any real answers, but below is a summary of what I read on the topic over the course of our sons' childhood and teenage years. The relevant books are listed in an appendix.

When our sons were small, I bought or borrowed quite a selection of books about being a parent. The different theories were rather overwhelming, but gradually I saw that there were some general themes. Most of the current authors in the late 1980s saw three broad 'styles' of parent: the authoritative, the authoritarian, and the permissive. Like the three bears' furniture in the classic fairy tale, these authors concluded that one style was too hard, one too soft, and the other just right.

Naturally I wanted to be a good parent, and it seemed logical that the mid-ground was the best way. I did not want to control my children's lives entirely; on the other hand, I had no desire for them to race around destroying things, yelling and causing chaos.

These authors made it all sound quite straightforward. Lay down some clear guidelines, they said. Be as flexible as you can in most of your parenting, and always willing to negotiate. But have some boundaries, and apply some kind of 'consequences' for violating them. These, I read, will vary depending on family circumstances, and the age and personality of the child in question. But we parents have to exert authority, these books told me, because we are older, wiser and have more experience of life.

The books also stressed the vital importance of unconditional love, and letting our children know how important they are to us. One author talked about filling 'emotional tanks'. Hug children, maintain eye contact, spend time with them, he stressed.

Other writers offered different suggestions. There were ways of speaking to children that gained their attention. There were ideas about respectfully communicating boundaries. The more I read, the more confusing it became.

When I started home educating, I read these books again, and discovered more. I was particularly interested in a writer who talked about finding our children's 'love languages'. Some children, he said, respond well to verbal affirmation. Some need a lot of hugs and physical closeness. Some feel loved when you do things for them, or when you give them small gifts. Some feel most loved when you spend one-on-one time with them.

Even the strictest of the parenting books stressed that our children must know that we love them, and

Parenting while Home Educating

will always do so. We might not like what they do, at times. We might sometimes have to act in ways that they think is unloving. But if we keep their emotional tanks full, and let them know in as many ways as we can that they matter to us, other concerns are likely to be less significant.

The other principle stressed by all these authors was the importance of boundaries. They can be as flexible as we choose, but there are some situations in which we have to say 'no' to our children, or prevent them from doing something. This might be an action that could be life-threatening. Most parents insist that their children are strapped into a car seat when travelling, for instance. We would not let toddlers run in the street unsupervised, and never when there is busy traffic.

Other boundaries might be for the sake of someone else, if — for instance — we have a child who tries to kick or bite other children. Or it might be a situation where our greater experience and forethought is at variance with our children's desires, and we have to ensure they do (or do not do) something.

That is not to say that we have to coerce our children, or yell at them until they co-operate. Nor should we attempt to manipulate them. For young toddlers, distraction usually works well. For many children, a simple explanation is sufficient. In some situations we can offer choices, and in many cases we can discuss options and come up with suitable solutions that everyone can accept.

Then there are children who refuse to accept boundaries. This can start as young as eighteen months old, a precursor to the so-called 'terrible two' phase when our children exert their independence. It is also likely to happen around puberty, when hormones are running rampant and our young teenagers or pre-teens go through another phase of increasing independence. Whereas two-year-olds can still often be distracted, teenagers are well beyond that level.

So these authors recommend — in different ways — that we follow the principle of 'consequences'. Unfortunately that word has come to be synonymous with punishment, in some circles. But in its original meaning, it simply refers to something that happens as a result of a prior action. If I don't get any sleep, the natural consequence is that I will be tired the next day. If I don't eat my dinner, the consequence is that I will be hungry. If a teenager gets drunk, the likely consequence is a hangover.

As adults we are also aware of what might be termed 'logical' consequences to many actions. If we do not turn up to work, we will not receive a paycheque, and might lose our job. If we turn to a life of crime, we may end up in jail.

Children, as these authors point out, do not have the life experience to know about natural or logical consequences. So part of our role is to educate our children about how life works: that we need to wear more clothes or turn up the heating on a cold day; that we need to sleep in order to be rested; that too much sugar or junk food can make us sick. And we may also need to impose 'logical' consequences, sometimes. These too (the theory goes) help children to learn how life works.

As an example of logical consequences, some of the authors I read believe in the importance of the occasional 'time out'. This happens when we separate a child from the rest of the family for a short period, to cool down. Some write persuasively about 'reality discipline' — creatively ensuring that, as we used to say,

Parenting while Home Educating

we 'let the punishment fit the crime'. Terminology is important: most authors I read in the 1980s and 1990s did not like the word 'punishment', as it sounds like revenge. 'Discipline' was the preferred word, related to the word 'disciple'. It implies something positive, at least as an outcome, as children learn and develop with the help of someone else.

It is said by some experts that children's brains develop gradually: in their early years they live in the moment and rarely think about the future. The ability to avoid temptation because of long-term negative consequences does not usually appear until the late teens or early twenties. For some individuals, it may never fully happen. Most of us experience lapses at times, procrastinating about important jobs even though we know we will regret it. But young children or teens, caught up in peer pressure, or any compulsive behaviour, may want — and need — a parent to make them stop.

It was only after we started home educating that I came across the theory of autonomous parenting. Some of the authors I read in the 1980s would call this 'permissive' or even 'neglectful' parenting, but proponents of the theory deny that. Children, the theory says, have inbuilt desires to be kind, to fit in with the world, to please their parents, and to learn. If we enable their desires, imposing few (or no) boundaries, they will naturally develop into the best people they can be.

However, this does not mean ignoring our children. Nor does it mean leaving doors open to the street, or dangerous things lying around. Naturally we must keep toddlers safe. That is an acceptable boundary, according to this theory, because children have an inherent desire to survive. So if we see a young child about to run in front of a car, it is fine to grab his hand to stop him.

With autonomous raising of children, parents have

to be fully involved with their children at all times. They need to explain why some things are dangerous. They should also exercise common sense. Autonomous parenting should not mean that children run out of control or rule the household, nor that they trample over their parents' wishes. If we do not want a lively child to break a crystal vase, we should not leave it where he can reach it.

Autonomous parenting theory teaches that there should be mutually acceptable solutions to any problem that arises. If two children want to play with the same toy, we encourage them to decide, together, whether they should play with it in turns, or together, or on alternate days, or whether they should save money and buy a second one. If four family members have different plans for a Saturday, and they cannot all be followed, then a family meeting is recommended. Open discussion should help them refine their ideas, listen to each other, and find ways to please everyone. The word 'compromise' is not encouraged, in this theory, because that tends to suggest nobody winning. It is particularly important to ensure that no one person gives up their wishes regularly for the sake of everyone else, as that can lead to resentment.

I liked this theory very much. In some respects, I naturally followed it and still believe in it. Certainly as far as education goes, I have found that, given their own space and time, children and teens tend to learn all they need to learn with little or no compulsion from outside.

However I have some reservations with autonomous parenting as I have also heard of families where it did not work well. Every child is different. Not all children are temperamentally kind and willing to please. Some are naturally self-centred, and if not guided appropriately

Parenting while Home Educating

can become quite selfish. Moreover, children who are natural pleasers can too easily give in to their more dominant siblings, and never have their wishes followed.

I know of many families who have set meal times and bedtimes for their children. These are boundaries which autonomous parenting adherents disagree with. But the kitchen can descend to chaos if every child eats whatever they like whenever they choose and leave dirty dishes on the table. Sometimes parents find that they need time to themselves, and children become cranky if they stay up too late, so bedtimes are imposed.

Discussion is good, and it is important to take children's preferences into account. But inevitably as parents our preferences influence what we buy, when we choose to eat, and when we like to have peace in the evenings. Our children's choices will reflect their upbringing and culture anyway, and a few boundaries imposed — with discussion, and the possibility of changes when appropriate — can help children learn to respect and appreciate others more.

The problem with any theory is that it can become a list of rules or requirements, with people asking what should happen under some (possibly unlikely) circumstances. It is not always easy to remember the details of a theory anyway.

I come back to my belief that each child is different, each family situation Is different, and all parents are different. Nobody can get everything right all the time. Parents make mistakes, and that's good: it helps children to see that they are human.

Here are some of my personal principles for parenting:

- Let your children know that you love them, in ways they appreciate, without embarrassing them.

- Listen to your children rather than assuming you know better. If the volume is too loud, or the language too crude, ask them to moderate it and then listen.
- Be willing to discuss any issue. Let each person brainstorm ideas and note them in a non-judgemental way. You do not need to let this descend into total silliness unless you are all enjoying doing so. If the matter is important, try to keep the discussion on track.
- Keep your children safe when they are small, but encourage older children to take age-appropriate risks (within the boundaries of care and common sense) if they want to, after a discussion about likely natural consequences.
- Expect the best from your children at all times. When it does not happen, do not allocate blame, but deal with whatever arises, and move on.
- If you have boundaries or house rules of any kind, be prepared to negotiate when appropriate. But while they are in place, stick to them. Fuzzy boundaries are very confusing for children.
- Start each day afresh.

Did I do all these things all the time? Of course not. But I still believe in them as ideals.

Our experience

While much of our home education worked along autonomous lines, we found that we were more comfortable with a few boundaries. We had a lot of discussion about tidiness, for instance. I wanted our living room to stay presentable. Our sons wanted to be able to leave things lying about.

They also said that they wanted to be able to keep their rooms as messy as they wished. I then stated that I was not happy about digging through their clutter to find dirty clothes. So we agreed that I would wash what they put in the laundry basket — but they would have to put up with having no clean clothes (a logical, agreed-upon consequence) if they had not done so.

They then accepted that if their rooms were their own responsibility, it was reasonable to keep the living room tidy. They said that I could confiscate anything I found lying around the living room. They also agreed that if they broke things, they would pay for repairs or replacement.

We discussed meals and planned menus together, my younger son offered to do some of the cooking, and they organised a rota system for setting and clearing the table. If they wanted to eat at a different time, due to some other commitment, we would decide together whether we all ate earlier (or later), or they made themselves something separately.

These are just examples. Every family — as I have said before — is different.

Epilogue to Part One

Pros and cons

In summary of the earlier chapters of this first section, here are some pros and cons of home education which may help you as you consider your options. This short chapter looks at some of the general pros and cons, in the hope that more parents will consider their options before enrolling their children in schools. I also hope that you will bear these in mind each year, as you discuss, with your children, whether to continue what you are doing, or try something different.

The balance will be different for each family, and for each child within a family. Much will depend, too, on where you live and what your local schools are like. The family structure is also relevant: for a single parent, or when both are working full time, home education is more difficult to arrange than when one parent is able to be home full-time.

Nevertheless, there are some general principles that should be considered when determining how your child will be educated.

Pros of home education

1. Individual attention and instruction. However you decide to go about home education, there is a higher adult-to-child ratio than there can be in a regular school. Even if you have three or four (or more) children at home, you can give far more attention to them than a teacher can with a large class, even if there is a teaching assistant or parent volunteer to help. With home education, you can tailor each child's education precisely, answering any questions as they come up.

2. Children work at their own pace. This is related to the first, but is from the child's perspective. Whereas a school may take a whole term to cover the topic of – for instance – solid geometry, or Ancient Rome – a child educated at home can learn about them in more diverse time periods. An hour or two may be sufficient to introduce a maths or history topic and cover all that is needed. Equally, it may take a year or more for a child to grasp something for which they are not yet ready.

    Learning to read is a good example of this. Some children learn to read as young as three or four, some not until they are nine or ten, or older. It does not matter! There is no shame in being a late reader, and no reason for pride in early readers. At home, education can be suited to a child's needs and abilities (as the law requires) and children can take as long as necessary to learn anything.

3. Children's interests can be followed. While some home educators choose to use a curriculum, or follow school subjects, there is still far more scope for encouraging children to follow their own interests, whatever they may be.

Epilogue to Part One 93

4. More time for relaxation. A typical school day lasts about seven hours, with – by the time a child is in the teens – two or three hours of homework each night. Even if home educators spend two or three hours on direct education (and many do not) there is still far more time for reading, music, board games, walks... or whatever appeals.
5. Flexibility with holidays. With education authorities becoming stricter about authorised absences, holidays or day trips in term time are almost impossible for children in school. With home education you can take a break whenever you wish, and take advantage of off-season travel or days out.
6. Lack of peer pressure. The teenage years can be stressful and depressing for teens who are bullied, or insecure in any way, or who feel that they do not fit in. Peer pressure can be devastating, leading some teens to experiment with dangerous lifestyles. Home educated children and teens are usually more confident in their abilities, and less prone to negative peer pressure.

Cons of home education

1. It can be expensive. Quite apart from the potential loss of income when a parent is home full-time, any textbooks, art supplies, writing materials, musical instruments, and so on must be paid for, rather than supplied by the school. If you decide to follow a curriculum, that can be pricey. If your children want to take GCSEs or A-levels, even if they can study them at home, there is a fee for every exam taken as a private student.
2. Possible lack of friends. While some children are friendly with neighbours, or take part in various

groups, it can sometimes be difficult to make close friends of their own age when educated at home. There are more opportunities of mixing with local people of all ages, and as discussed in a previous chapter, home educated children in general have no problem socialising when the opportunities arise. But it cannot be denied that home education can feel isolating, if you have an only child, or live in an area where there are no other home educating families.

3. Home education is full-time for one or more parents. Many of us love having children around, but it can be tiring and overwhelming never to have time to oneself. Home education is a full-time job. Even if you follow a curriculum and choose set hours of the day for structured education, questions may arise at any time of day or night. As when looking after a toddler, parents are never off-duty when home educating.

4. Disapproval of relatives and friends. It can sometimes be hard for grandparents, who may be worried that your children are missing out on educational experiences or other aspects of schooling. Friends whose children are in school may take offence, thinking that you see yourself as superior to them. Discussion is usually helpful, and as time goes by, these facets usually become easier. But they can be difficult to overcome when you first start home educating.

5. Dealing with the Local Education Authority. While home education is legal throughout the UK, some LEA officials try to monitor or advise, even if you do not want them to. Some LEAs are fine, and may be helpful. But you might have to deal with officials

who do not like your style of education and who may then do all they can to get your children into school.
6. Further education applications can be complex. Although many home educated students go on to university, the process is likely to be less straightforward if they have not taken A-levels. In addition, they do not have careers advisors to help, nor do they have Head teachers to give an academic reference.

Conclusion

I have tried to be fair, giving six potential advantages of home education, and six possible disadvantages. Whether or not any of these are relevant to you will depend on your own educational philosophy, as well as the characters and needs of your children.

However, if your child is being bullied, or finds school life impossible for any reason, please consider home education for at least a year or so. No decision has to be permanent, and most of the disadvantages listed above are not relevant when home educating for short periods.

Part Two

Of making many books there is no end, and much study wearies the body.

Ecclesiastes 12: 12b, Bible, NIV

Prologue to Part Two

Home Education and Subjects

It can be tempting, when starting home education, to think in terms of core academics, as if emulating school education: English, maths, history and so on. That is because subjects such as these have traditionally been considered essential for a well-rounded person.

But is this correct? Are the needs of today's young people the same as ours were? Latin used to be compulsory in all good schools. Nowadays it is almost impossible to find a school that teaches Latin outside the private sector. On the other hand, ICT was not a subject when I was at school; the idea of home computers was laughable. But technology and computer skills are widely accepted as important even for primary school children today.

There have been rapid changes due to the advances in technology over the past few decades, but these have not yet reached a plateau. How will society change in the next twenty years? This can be a good discussion topic with your children, and is important to bear in mind as you consider how you will educate them.

Maths in primary schools in the middle of the 20th

century used to begin with extensive, often tedious arithmetic. When my sons were in school in the 1990s, concepts and different topics were introduced at young ages. Arithmetic was seen in a wider context, and children were taught to think in mathematical terms and see connections rather than learn arithmetical facts.

History, a hundred years ago, was taught with lists of dates and famous people. Nowadays it is taught topically in schools. Modern history text books help children to understand how people lived, and what life would have been like in different periods. Children are encouraged to think about the reasons behind wars and revolutions.

In recent decades, educational styles have changed rapidly. In the late 1990s, the UK government decided that basic literacy and numeracy were being neglected in primary schools. They saw that British children were falling behind their counterparts in other parts of the world. So they introduced 'literacy hour' and 'numeracy hour'.

Children from the age of about seven were expected to do rapid mental arithmetic, with regular paper tests to see how well they did. English teaching altered, too; no longer were children grouped by ability, but expected to discuss literature or grammar as a class. As for teaching reading, successive governments have determined that phonics, whole words, or (more recently) synthetic phonics must be taught. Different governments change the rules and the expectations.

As with most educational decisions, each of these innovations has worked well for some children, and badly for others. No doubt teaching styles will continue to change as future governments introduce new ideas, only to discover after a few years that they work no better than the previous ones.

I mention all this as an encouragement to new home educators. Even when you think things are going terribly, and feel as if you are not providing what your children need, they may still be doing better than they would at your local school.

A school is an organisation, bound by legal regulations and its own style of working. Any organisation must have rules and a purpose in order to keep going. But there is not much room for flexibility. A Year Two class teacher will expect to teach much the same curriculum year after year, despite the fact that an entirely different set of children will arrive each September. If Ancient Egyptians are being studied in the spring term, then that's what will happen every year, whether or not the children are interested.

A family functions more like an organism which grows and changes over time. It can take account of individuals, and their needs and desires. If your children are passionate about Ancient Egypt, then they can learn as much as they want to about the topic, irrelevant of what term or year it is. If they are not interested, then even if you follow a formal curriculum, or want them to learn about the full spread of history, you can touch on the topic lightly and move on.

As explained in the first section, there are many different ways of educating children at home. You can follow a formal curriculum, or you can take each day as it comes, going along with whatever interests the children. You can timetable hours for education, or you can treat the whole of your children's life as educational. You can think about different subjects, as happens in schools, or you can merge everything into one.

This section of the book is for home educators, particularly those with younger children, who would like to introduce different topics within the concept of different subjects. It does not go into any depth, but gives a flavour of what you might do. In places I give some of our own experiences; as with personal commentary in the first section, these are examples of how home education worked for us. They are not intended to be prescriptive.

The aim of these subject-related chapters is primarily to help new home educators to become more confident. If you want to think in terms of subjects, and would like some ideas about how to cover them while home educating, you may find some useful tips. You will probably have thought of many of them already; I am not offering anything new. But I hope it will be reassuring to realise that ordinary life can provide an adequate education.

If at any point you try something suggested in these pages, and realise that it is not working, or is not appropriate, then please stop using it. I offer ideas based on my own experiences, and those of other home educating friends. If something helps, that's great. If not, then the best thing is to move on to something different.

Note, too, that this section of the book offers a starting point only, and is more relevant to young children than teenagers. You can find rather more about some of these topics on the home-ed.info site. There are additional links on the site to further information if your child wants to take the subjects to deeper levels.

The final chapter of this section is about exams and university. These are more relevant to those with teenagers, or who want to take a long-term view of home education.

CHAPTER SEVEN
Maths

Maths for younger children

Some adults recall their least favourite subject at school being mathematics. Perhaps they did not understand the concepts of what numbers stand for when they were taught about the symbols and had to learn how to manipulate them. Perhaps they understood very well, and were bored with drill and busywork. Or perhaps they simply did not like the teacher.

Maths, in essence, relates to the underlying structure of the world, which we see in patterns, shapes, quantities and intelligent guesses. Numbers are an important part of it, but only to help us calculate or quantify.

Home education is ideal for learning maths because children can do so at their own pace. They can progress in their preferred styles, learning in practical ways appropriate to their needs. Yet many parents are nervous about helping their children with this subject, possibly due to their own negative experiences. This may be why so many use maths workbooks, even if their general home educating style is more relaxed. If books of this kind inspire your children and help them to enjoy maths, that's great. But they are not essential.

Until the age of at least seven or eight (and, perhaps, later), most learning will happen by osmosis through everyday life. Beyond that, it depends very much on the child's interest. So long as basic concepts of numbers are understood, calculators and computers can be used to deal with complex arithmetic and lengthy calculations. I believe it is important for children to know how to weigh and measure, and to deal with money. With these skills they should be able to cope adequately with adult life even if they never learn any formal geometry or algebra.

Starting when your children are young, it is a good idea to use correct mathematical language where appropriate. You can talk about what you are doing when you are involved in something arithmetical. Count apples, or stairs, or books from the library, for instance. You can talk about numbers as you might talk about animals or colours.

There is no need to teach young children to recite numbers by rote. Indeed, it is best to introduce the numbers gradually, in everyday conversation. You can explain, for instance, that when you have one apple, and pick up another apple, you have two apples. You can show that something similar happens with bananas, or biscuits. You can talk in this style about socks or shoes, or anything else that typically comes in pairs. Do not worry about making this into a formal learning experience. If your child does not seem to understand, then perhaps they are not yet ready to do so.

If your children are older and you did not use this kind of language when they were little, it is not too late. With home education there are always more opportunities for learning, and there are no rules about when a child should know certain things. You may find that your older child has picked up these concepts anyway. If not, find ways to introduce them at an appropriate level for their age and development.

When your child knows about 'one' and 'two', and is familiar with how items can be grouped in this way, you can introduce another important idea. They know that one shoe and another shoe are two shoes. But one shoe plus one sock is... one shoe plus one sock. When your children realise that, they have grasped a basic and important algebraic concept. If they realise that one shoe plus one sock is exactly the same as one sock plus one shoe, then they have understood the basic nature of the so-called 'commutative property'. This is a pre-algebraic concept usually taught in secondary schools.

You do not, of course, have to introduce these topics before talking about other numbers. If this is your first child, then 'three' is another useful number. There are three of you in the family. A bigger family may have three children. Or perhaps your child has three teddies, or has put three trucks in a row. Instead of simply counting abstractly, you can show one teddy, then two teddies together, then three of them, giving the numbers as you do so. Again, only do this if your child is interested. Some children might want to do this again and again, others might grab the teddies and move away. Signals of this kind are an important indication of your child's interest level, and it is always best to respect them.

Other numbers can be introduced as appropriate, in concrete ways. If, like me, you tend more towards thinking than talking, it can feel a bit artificial to make deliberate conversation about what seems like trivialities. But they are not trivial to your child, who is learning all the time. So you can say, even though it is obvious to you, something like: 'We usually put out two plates for lunch, because it's just you and me. Two people. But Granny is coming today, so that's one more person. One, two, three plates. Granny, Mummy, you.'

The reverse of addition is subtraction. A young child does not need these words; instead he needs to see them as connected concepts. If you have used simple adding language as suggested above, then simple 'taking away' language will probably come naturally. If you have two biscuits and you eat one of them, you have one left. If you are wearing two shoes and take one of them off, you are wearing one shoe. If you are a family of four people and one person goes out, then three of you are left at home. If you have borrowed four library books and take two of them back, you still have two.

Do not even suggest that subtraction is more difficult than addition (or, when you get to it, that multiplication or division are harder still). They are all basic concepts and are inter-related. If you have three people and each of them has two cakes, you can count the cakes to find that there are six. The six cakes are shared between three people and each person has two. If you want to share out six cakes between two people, they each get three. If three are eaten, there are three left.

There is no need to do more than mention these things as they happen, and answer any questions your child might have. Practical situations like these help arithmetic concepts to settle in your child's mind. They do not need to see the symbols 2 and 3 until they fully understand what 'two-ness' and 'three-ness' mean: that two apples are totally unlike two elephants, but they share a common property, that of being 'two'.

As your child gradually learns about numbers, there

are counting songs or rhymes you can use to help remember the order. There are also many picture books featuring numbers up to ten. Some simply show pictures of items to count, some have stories attached, whether about a hungry caterpillar or hippos coming to visit, or elephants crammed in a large bed. Reading and talking about number-related books will help your child understand the progress of the first ten numbers without any pressure. But let your children help to choose the reading material. If they have no interest in number-related books, put them aside for another day.

There are plenty of toys for young children which introduce the idea of shapes. A classic toy, which has many variations, has holes in different shapes and matching plastic or wooden blocks to be pushed through the holes. I recall a kind of 'post box' with holes in the lid for posting the shapes through. But today's child rarely posts a letter, so modern posting toys are more likely to be made in other shapes, perhaps related to favourite books or TV shows.

Whether or not your child has a toy of this kind (and they can often be found in charity shops) you can talk about shapes naturally as you see them. A photo might be square, the TV screen is a rectangle, a coin is round. Your dining table might be round, or oblong; Granny's might be a rectangle. While you can keep the vocabulary simple, some children like learning the correct words once they are aware of different kinds of shape. The three-dimensional shape of a whole book is a cuboid (or rectangular prism). A square, with equal length edges, is a specific kind of rectangle. Dice are cubes. A clock face is a circle, a toilet roll a cylinder. And so on. Once a child knows some of the relevant words, they may like pointing out the shapes they spot when you are out.

Words like 'big' and 'small' are mathematical ones too, and the ability to compare sizes is an important one. It is obvious to you that a big packet of biscuits contains more than a small packet, but not necessarily to your young child. You probably naturally talk about phrases such as 'too heavy' or that you have 'too many' books to fit on one shelf. All these are mathematical concepts which your child will grasp easily if you use them informally, as part of everyday language.

You can talk about patterns that you observe, too, in nature, or in the home. You could show your child how to sort toy bricks by shape, or size, or colour. Some children naturally do these things, and it can be fun to see them discover colours or patterns on their own. If they do not do so, you can show them how you can pick up two red bricks, or that this one is bigger than that one. You can also demonstrate that a block on top of another block is higher than one on its own.

At some point your children may ask about number symbols. Perhaps they spot them in a book, or you see them on houses. You can talk about why we use numbers and what they mean. Make sure you explain that the numbers are a kind of shorthand for the concept, not anything mystical in themselves. If you introduce the arithmetic symbols, explain that '2+2=4' is an easier way of writing something like: 'If we have two elephants and then another two elephants arrive to join them, there will be four elephants altogether'.

Some children like to invent their own arithmetic symbols. If your child wants to draw a little picture to represent the apples or elephants after each number, that is fine. It is a form of simple algebra, which needs to be understood intuitively before arithmetic can make sense.

Words help with concepts, and a young child will learn almost endlessly from parental conversation. The theory of allowing a child to explore and discover everything on his own is a good one. But no child can experience every possibility in life, and each child's discoveries and choices will inevitably be guided by what their parents or other carers can offer. If you can naturally use simple mathematical terms, as you would use other words in conversation, your child's understanding will expand appropriately.

Maths for older children

If you have introduced your child to simple number concepts, adding and taking away small numbers, then at some point they are likely to want to know more. Trust your instincts as you introduce or talk about new concepts. If you are comfortable with mathematical words, then this will probably come naturally. But if you disliked or distrusted numbers and maths at school, it may be more difficult.

You could, for instance, introduce the idea and vocabulary of basic fractions when your child is comfortable with at least the first few numbers, and simple adding and subtracting. Cut an apple into two pieces, and explain that each one is a half. Two half apples are one whole apple. Likewise, two half cakes are one whole cake. When your child is familiar with this idea, you could explain that half of a half is called a quarter. A cake can be cut into two halves, four or quarters. Then show your children (if they do not work it out for themselves) how two quarters are the same as a half.

Similarly, depending on how many people there are in your family, or at the table, you can talk about thirds or fifths, when dividing a cake or pie. These basic fractional concepts are part of our language. Children who struggle with fractions at school may be confused by the notation because they have never really understood what basic fractions refer to.

Lego (or similar construction toys) can be used to demonstrate how some fractions work, alongside basic division. Do not deliberately set out to teach a maths lesson, but take opportunities when appropriate. For instance, you can lay an 8-length brick alongside two 4-bricks, or build three 4-bricks (or four 3-bricks) end to end on top of a single 12-brick. A child who grasped the commutative principle of addition when he was younger may spot at once that four 3-bricks are the same length as three 4-bricks.

If your child is frustrated that his building bricks do not come in lengths of five or seven, it might be getting hold of (or make) some Cuisenaire rods. The simplest ones are a set of small wooden blocks of different colours, with lengths from one to ten. This is a popular educational tool that can be used for discovering many arithmetical properties, often used by home educators and increasingly in schools.

There are also lots of children's board games which involve simple arithmetic skills. Some use the number symbols for path-following or counting games such as Snakes and Ladders or Ludo. A slightly older child might like money-oriented games like Monopoly (which has a junior version for small children). Card games, Dominoes, Yahtzee!, and many others can aid young children in acquiring number skills in the context of fun. Perhaps more importantly, games can help them see for themselves that it is useful to be able to manipulate numbers with confidence.

Estimation is a useful skill, which children can develop with everyday discussion and construction toys. When you bake, you probably use scales to weigh ingredients or (if you prefer American recipes) cups to measure them. Depending on the age of your child, that can lead to a discussion of the metric vs imperial system, or the accuracy of modern scales. That might then lead to online research into how people used to weigh things before digital weighing was possible.

Other mathematical topics are likely to arise naturally from activities your children do. If not, and if this worries you, then you might discuss with them why it is useful to have some basic maths skills, and look together for a book or website which appeals to you all. But keep it low-key and never insist on worksheets or repetition of skills they have already mastered, unless you have a child who likes this kind of structure. Maths is not supposed to be dull.

If your child struggles with basic arithmetic, but wants to be able to add or multiply, buy a calculator and show your child how to use it. More important than manipulating numbers is to understand how to cope with everyday problems — dealing with money, sharing out food, doubling recipes, measuring, and so on, and how to use the calculator to find the results. Teenagers with smartphones should be able to use them for any calculations they might need.

However, it is a good idea to help older children understand the importance of estimating. That way, they can have an idea of what kind of answer they might get, and can re-check their figures if their calculator gives something that is far too big (or far too small).

If you want to ensure that your child covers basic maths skills, including arithmetic, in a more formal manner, you can do this without inducing boredom, so long as you teach concepts rather than merely facts. Numbers are all inter-related, and a child who understands this will usually be able to work out ways of doing arithmetic, even if not at the rapid speed of someone who has been drilled in mental arithmetic. But a child who understands numbers is more likely to find interesting ways of solving problems, and to enjoy maths in general.

Some older children, given the freedom to learn in their own way, will rapidly understand quite complex mathematics and will enjoy solving problems and learning new techniques. But others are not gifted in this way. We would not expect our teens to play a sport they hated, or force them to study a musical instrument they found tedious. It makes no sense that many parents (and, indeed, schools) insist that maths must be continued long past the stage where a child finds it useful or interesting.

One of the objections I have heard to home education is along the lines of, 'I couldn't possibly teach my teenager any algebra or geometry. I never understood them myself at school.' It seems a fair comment. Except that, if you did not understand these concepts in school, why do you suppose that your child would do any better? Problems with mathematical concepts may run in the family. Besides, as an adult, have you needed geometry or algebra?

While these topics can be fun for those who enjoy maths, they are of little use in most careers. If an older child struggles with advanced maths, my suggestion would be to abandon the subject. Perhaps you could think of it on a par with learning to speak a little-known language: useful for some people, fun for linguists, but irrelevant for the majority.

If at some stage in the future your child wants a career

where these skills are essential, the motivation will be there. Study is likely to be less painful at this stage than if it is forced because of someone else's pre-planned agenda. A teenager can take an adult education course when he is sixteen or even eighteen, if necessary, or take an extensive mathematical skills class with other people who find it difficult.

I say all this as someone who mostly enjoyed maths at school. I loved algebra and calculus, but I was aware even then that I would probably never use them in real life. I went on to study maths at university, and worked for some years as a computer programmer. I needed to think logically; but I have never needed most of those maths skills I had liked so much at school.

When, in adult life, I have needed to calculate prices and sizes of carpets, or balance our bank account, I use a calculator or computer software. I need the conceptual awareness of how bank accounts work, and to understand bookkeeping at a basic level. But those skills were not covered in my school, nor in my degree. Instead I learned them at home in a few minutes when I realised how important it was to keep track of our finances.

So there is no need to panic about home educating your teenager if you do not have much of a grasp of secondary school maths. The best thing is to brainstorm with your children what kind of maths they might need for their chosen careers, if they have thought about them. Discuss what they would like to know. Think about the kinds of problems they might need to solve, either now or when they are older. Help them with strategies for problem-solving. Involve them in your household budgeting, baking, shopping and house decorating. Take a day at a time, and if your child asks a question you cannot answer, turn to your library or the Internet and, if necessary, help them with research skills.

The more you and your children think of maths as a part of everyday life, the more likely they are to be intrigued and want to know more. It is only when we become afraid, bored, or bemused that we tend back away from something and feel unable to learn.

To sum up: your teenagers will not necessarily understand maths if they go to school anyway. If they do not naturally have much aptitude for the subject, they may instead learn to dislike and avoid it if forced to take a maths course. If you — or your home educated children — feel that they need to know more maths, but they are not learning from one method, try another. Or else put it aside for a while, and they may then understand more easily a few months later. There are many interesting books or sites that cover different angles of maths, which you may find helpful. Perhaps your teenagers could take a programming course. Or maybe you could look together at maths in music or art.

All education should be fulfilling and worthwhile. In general it should also enjoyable, fitting in with the children's interests and motivation, as well as their abilities and aptitudes.

CHAPTER EIGHT
Reading and Writing

When the National Curriculum was introduced in the UK, English at primary level was divided into five sections:

Speaking and Listening, Reading, Handwriting, Creative Writing, and Spelling and Grammar.

You do not, of course, have to follow any curriculum, and the exact words have changed in the past decade or so. But as broad categories, these sections cover useful concepts and skills, which are relevant to learning and life. This chapter should help you see that they are easily developed as part of home education.

Speaking and Listening

At home with your children, you have plenty of opportunity to listen and speak with them. You can encourage them to express their feelings and ask questions at any time. Even if you are not naturally chatty, you can talk with your children about places you go, or shows you have seen on television, or people you have met.

You probably read aloud to your children already. In home education you have the ideal opportunity to read plenty of books aloud. You can introduce your children to classics at an early age. You can read myths and legends, or stories connected with topics your children are studying. If you are not already members of a local library, this is a good time to join one. Talk together about what you read after you've finished a chapter. Children learn a great deal of vocabulary intuitively but there may be words they did not understand, or concepts they had not grasped.

Some ideas that are specifically taught in schools can be covered easily at home in general discussion. For instance, schoolchildren are expected to know about synonyms (words with similar meaning) and antonyms (the formal word for opposites). In our family, we found it interesting to talk, sometimes, about words that meant much the same as each other. We debated at length about subtle variations between similar words. The dictionary often came out at mealtimes when someone wanted to know the exact definition of a word, or to find its opposite.

Part of this feature of English in schools involves taking part in group drama. This is not so easy at home, particularly if you have only one or two children, or if they are widely different in age. However you may find that they will spontaneously develop their own play worlds with teddies or dolls, or tiny Lego people. Nancy Wallace in her excellent book 'Better than School' (no longer in print) describes her two home educated children having ongoing play sessions in which they developed an entire micro-world full of different characters. They created laws, conducted trade, and explored in mini-dramas related to topics the children were learning about.

I found that my children, over time, played similar games. When they were four or five, their worlds were full of teddies and other soft toys with a hierarchy of kings and queens and princes. As they grew older, an ever-increasing Lego city developed. They also invented games involving knights and castles and dragons. Other worlds were full of space ships. Our sons and their friends would spend hours acting out mini dramas and sagas. I have observed other home educating children playing in similar ways.

Do not be tempted to dismiss this as 'just' playing. Take time to listen, without being too obvious, and you may learn a lot about what currently interests your children. You may be surprised to discover what they have learned in recent weeks through books or circumstances. Children learn to speak in different ways and pretend to be adults through the tiny characters in their worlds. Conflict resolution and problem-solving can be played out in non-threatening ways, so there is no need to worry if their worlds sometimes appear rather more violent than you would like.

Beginning to write

If you give your children pencils and crayons from a young age, they are likely to make loops and swirls, big and small pictures, and to find the whole process enjoyable. As they get a little older, they will probably love to see you write their names, or a title for their pictures. At some point, they will probably want to imitate you. Learning to write may be as simple as that.

On the other hand, a child may ask to learn to write 'properly'. Some children like to learn in a structured way, and it is important to listen to their needs. There are many pre-writing books with mazes, patterns and puzzles for young children to try — just browse your local bookshop for some ideas, and see which ones appeal. If you want to teach your child to write without using workbooks, it is generally best to start with lowercase words (with an initial capital, if relevant) rather than uppercase letters.

It is also a good idea to help your children to form the letters correctly from the beginning. Most looped letters (such as a,c,d,e,g etc) are formed anti-clockwise, lines (as in b,i,l,k etc) from top to bottom. It is not wrong to form them in other ways, and some children do not want to be shown standard ways. But if your child wants to learn to write fast, or to join up the letters, it will be more awkward if they have not learned to form letters in the conventional way.

Some children quickly learn to make neat letters, others will find it much more difficult. If your children have difficulties with fine motor skills, make sure they have plenty of crayons to draw with, construction toys to build with, plasticine or play-dough to knead and other activities to strengthen the fingers. Keep handwriting sessions, if you have them, brief and enjoyable. If relevant, encourage your children to label their drawings, or to write brief notes to grandparents or friends. Whatever you do, never make writing into a chore.

At some point, many children want to join up their letters. If you feel that they need more of a guide than you can give, you could buy a handwriting text book and help to them follow the instructions. Again, keep the sessions brief, unless the child is highly motivated and wants to keep going. If they have no problem in developing a writing style, and want to practise handwriting, they might like to find a book of poems or fables which they could copy out and illustrate.

In these high-technology days most children will grow up not needing to write very much. So if your child dislikes writing or finds it difficult, they can still communicate via a computer or tablet. But handwriting is a useful fine motor skill, and being able to write legibly may be important. So while handwriting is no longer an essential skill to teach at a young age, it is worth encouraging if only so that your children can jot down notes for shopping lists, or write labels on parcels.

Creative writing

Some children want to write stories almost as soon as they can hold a pencil, their imagination flowing and running riot. Places you have been, stories you have read, people you meet: these may all provide inspiration for a story. If your child does not come up with their own ideas, but is keen to write, talk about the kind of thing they would like to produce and encourage them to get started. If they find typing easier than writing, then let them use a word processor. There is no need for a special child-friendly one: just set your regular one with biggish text and a clear font, and show your child how to use it.

To learn other writing styles, you could suggest that your child write (or type) letters. It can be fun to spend time on birthday thank-you letters, if you do them together. You can help your child understand how to write for a different audience. Granny is probably not interested in the same things as a best friend, for instance. You can explain how to set out a letter, and how to make it interesting. For variation, you could help your child to draft and write more formal letters — perhaps making a complaint, or applying for a free offer on the side of a cereal packet. If your child has strong opinions about a toy or other item that has recently been acquired, you could help them write (or dictate) a review on a relevant website.

Once your child writes with some confidence, you might want to use one of the many language books used in schools for more inspiration. While they are not essential and many home educated children never use them, we found some of them to be quite inspiring. The kind of books we liked had short excerpts from literature, with comprehension questions, some quizzes and observation, and ideas for creative writing. There is a wide variety available: check your local bookshops or library.

There are some children who show no interest in writing at any age. They may never want to write stories, either by hand or on the computer. They may dislike the idea of producing neat script, let alone anything joined up, and consider thank-you letters to be a form of torture. In school, this would be a problem; but at home it does not matter. You do not need your children to write in order to find out whether they have learned anything. Nor do they have to take any tests or exams, unless they choose to. If you worry that they might need to write at some point, you could always play games that encourage simple writing (such as 'hangman') or ask for help with your shopping list.

Eventually the majority of children will discover the importance of communicating in this way, if only by whatever is the preferred form of text messaging when they are teenagers. They are also likely to want to type at least basic information on computers or tablets, so long as you leave them to do it in their own time, in their own way. As they grow older, most children develop better fine motor control anyway. You may discover that a child who hated the thought of writing at the age of nine or ten can at least jot down notes or even write an essay four or five years later.

Spelling
Some children can spell intuitively by looking at a word and knowing whether it is correct or not. Others will start

by spelling somewhat phonetically, and gradually learn to spell correctly over the years, with a bit of assistance. Still others may learn rule after rule, and then still apply some of them wrongly. ('Why isn't rough spelt like cuff? Flight like kite?').

If your child is one of the last type, you will need to find a compromise between ignoring the problem completely and making it out to be all-important. Spelling is useful in helping us communicate in writing, but it is not a moral imperative. Nobody should feel bad about an inability to spell. It is no more their fault than being unable to sing in tune, or to catch a ball. Practice may help develop some skill, but not necessarily.

Unfortunately, however, incorrect spelling can make a writer seem ignorant, or not to be taken seriously. For a young child who is interested in writing and would like to spell better, you could teach some phonic rules. It is best to do these one at a time, without pressure, and help your child to spell words correctly. When you come across the many exceptions to phonic rules, let them know you agree they become frustrated. It is annoying that English is such an unpredictable language as far as spelling goes. The reason is partly to do with the many roots of our language (some Latin, some Greek, some Anglo-Saxon, and more...). If your child is interested in ancient civilisations, a study of etymology may come in useful. But do not push it: learning endless phonic rules may confuse them even more.

If your children want weekly spelling tests like schoolchildren have, then choose words which they often misspell and help them to practise writing them in sentences. Do not do this if they find it stressful, or if they become anxious about spelling as a result: anxiety is not conducive to learning. However if they enjoy this (and some children do) it may be a useful exercise for a while.

Do not worry if your child keeps making mistakes. Show them how to use the spell-checker on the computer or tablet. They may find that spelling improves as they get used to seeing correct spellings of words on the screen. One of my sons found spelling tests immensely stressful in school, and was convinced he could not spell. Within a year or two of home education, after regularly typing with a spell-checker enabled, his spelling ability had reached 'normal' age-appropriate levels.

Once your child is confident in all areas of English, they may want to write articles for magazines, or poetry, or short stories, or even full-length novels. They may want to write reviews online, or keep a blog. While you would need to be responsible for any online writing (and register in your name) if your child is under the age of thirteen, there is no reason why a child of any age should not write or type as much as they want to.

With modern print-on-demand publication, a child could even produce a printed book, illustrating the cover, and learning useful desktop publishing skills at the same time. You do not need to be limited by classroom times or anything other than your child's motivation and imagination.

Reading

Even the most relaxed of autonomous home educating parents can become a bit worried if a child does not — however slowly — learn to read. There are a wide variety of ages at which children start this skill, however. In schools, most children start recognising or sounding out words, with assistance, around the age of five or six. It is expected that they can read fluently by the time they are about eight to ten. But a few children learn to read (usually without much teaching) before they reach compulsory education age, and some may still be struggling when they finish primary school.

With home education, there is even more of a range. Home educated children do not have to read in order to learn; parents can read aloud to them, or they can discuss issues, or work with their hands. This is in contrast to a classroom where it is vital to have children reading to understand new concepts or information.

People interested in home education often ask about reading, and how to teach it. It can be easy to feel that we must be doing something wrong if our child does not read by the age of around eight or nine. Concerned relatives may challenge home educators whose children are not yet reading. It can be confusing. We know in theory that home education is more efficient than school learning. So it seems odd that quite a number of home educated children are 'behind' in this important skill. If a child shows no interest in learning to read, we might start to wonder if we are raising an illiterate person.

Part of the problem is that children do not learn to read entirely naturally. Give a young toddler a few books, and they are more likely to chew the corners than to ask you how to decode the printed squiggles. It is only if you read regularly to your child from babyhood that they realise that they can turn the pages and look at the pictures. Even then, while some children intuitively make the connection between the printed words and the story, others do not.

Some children become aware of printed words in everyday life at a young age. They might ask you what road signs or leaflets say, and make the leap of understanding that words on a page or screen are a form of communication. But other children ignore them completely. This is a personality or learning style difference, not a measure of intelligence. You could think of it as similar to the way that some children are fascinated by the workings of a car or washing machine, while others barely notice them.

Can reading be learned as easily as speaking? It would appear so, for a small percentage of children whose minds work that way. But even then, there has to be some parental input. Children do not learn to speak unless other people talk to them. When our babies start making babbling noises, we interpret them, giving instant feedback and — later on — gentle non-directive correction.

When you read to your children regularly, they may be fascinated by words. They might start asking you what the words say, perhaps even making their own attempts at reading them. For a young child, simply answering questions is sufficient. You do not need to talk about sounds or phonics or even letters when a child asks what a word says. If they have the ability to read at a young age, they will almost certainly also have the ability to build up their own internal phonics system. This is rather like the way toddlers develop their own internal grammar system for spoken language without ever being taught about verbs or tenses.

Sometimes young children like adults to run a finger along the words as they read, so that they can make the connections as they hear the words. For some children, this is enough: a few more questions, a bit of playing around with words and perhaps letters (such as magnetic fridge letters) and they will be reading.

Children who learn this way may not have the ability to sound out words in traditional style. They may not even 'hear' how words work at first, if they are primarily visually orientated. But there are children who can and do learn to read like this, and who tend to become rapid and fluent readers at a young age. Children who have this kind of mind will learn to read without any direct teaching, so long as you provide the basic resources. These include picture books with simple words, and the example of older children and adults reading for enjoyment. Most importantly, they need regular periods when stories are read aloud to them, and a natural discussion of written words in everyday life.

Is this a good thing? Should parents try and push their children into reading at a young age by asking leading questions? I don't think so. Children who read at a very young age may miss out on other activities, and some experts believe it can have a bad effect on eyesight. Early-reading children may have poorer co-ordination or motor skills than their more active peers. You cannot stop a child who wants to learn to read when they are just two or three years old, but there is no need to persuade a small child to recognise words or letters if they show no interest in doing so.

At some point, however, most children will show interest in learning to read. If they are not early visually orientated readers, they will probably need the help of phonics. These are, essentially, the sounds made by individual letters, and combinations such as ch or th. English is not a phonetic language, and there are many words that must be learned by sight only, but a basic grasp of the broad phonic rules is useful. There are many books which cover them extensively, if you do not feel confident or if your child wants some structured reading lessons.

To introduce phonics at home, you could try making large coloured cards with letters on them (lowercase is best to start with) or use magnetic fridge letters. At first, you could show your child how to make their name, and the names of other people in the family. You could tell them the names of the letters, if they are interested, or the sounds they make, if you prefer.

If your child is eager to read, you could make simple words like 'cat' or 'pig' from these letters. Then play a game where you choose a different letter to make new words — like 'hat' or 'big'. Some young children love nonsense words, so show them imaginary words as well — like 'zat'. Our children enjoyed Dr Seuss books such as 'Fox in Socks' or 'The Cat in the Hat' which are full of real and nonsense words to encourage playing around with words and phonics.

As your child begins to sound out or recognise a good selection of basic words, make sure they have some very easy-to-read books with interesting stories, and read them together. Encourage your child to read a page, but help them out immediately when they get stuck. Never insist that they sound out a word unless they want to. Instead, help them to guess from context or from the initial sound, and always tell them the word if they start to get worried. You want them to enjoy the story and want to read more, not to be proficient immediately. They may want to read the same book over and over, or they may want you to read alternate pages. It does not matter. So long as your child is trying to read, and enjoying it, they will continue.

If you do not have a lot of picture books, charity shops are a great source of inexpensive ones. If you have a local library, it is worth going regularly — weekly if possible, so that your children can choose whatever books they like from the junior sections. Some libraries have activities for young children which encourage reading, and which may introduce books you would not have thought of.

Once your children can read with some confidence, all you need to do is to tell them how to pronounce words which they don't know, if asked, and help them find out the meanings of words they do not understand. Provide plenty of fiction and non-fiction, and encourage free choice of books from the library. I would also recommend that you continue reading to your children long beyond the time when they are fluent, if they still enjoy it. Reading aloud helps to keep children's vocabulary and understanding ahead of their actual reading ability. We read to our sons until our older one left home; this way we could start them off on new series, and inspire them to read our own childhood and teenage favourites. But note that some children do not enjoy hearing books read aloud, and resist attempts to read to them after they can read for themselves.

There is no need to worry if your newly reading children seem to want a steady diet of what you consider junk fiction, or even comics. So long as they associate reading with enjoyment, they will continue to read for pleasure. Most children will attempt more advanced books in their own time, particularly if you are still reading to them regularly.

If your older children do not read for themselves, you may worry that they will never learn at home. It is important to stay patient and not to pressurise. Keep reading to them and they will almost certainly want to read for themselves eventually. If your child has a learning problem like dyslexia then they will find it considerably more difficult, and you may need specialist help. However, if there is no learning difficulty, then reading will happen sooner or later, and is all the more enjoyable if it happens according to the child's own schedule.

Grammar and Punctuation

Language consists of words — spoken or written — which we use to communicate with other people. Grammar is the structure of that language: the way it is used, and the conventions that help us understand what is meant from the context. We learn grammar informally as toddlers when we learn to speak. If you speak correctly it is likely that your children will too.

Small children seem to have an intuitive grasp of language structure. This is why they sometimes make mistakes, assuming principles that are not always true. If you hear a child talk about 'two mouses' he is not repeating something he has heard; he has understood the concept that we add the sound '-es' to a word ending in the 's' sound, to create a plural. If he says, 'the two mouses runned away', you know he has also understood that to create a past tense we usually add the ending '-ed' to a verb.

There is no need to correct a child who uses unconventional (though logical) forms like this. They will gradually learn the exceptions as they grow up. However, non-directive responses demonstrating accurate grammar can be helpful, such as, 'Yes, the two mice ran away'. This is how most grammar is absorbed when we are young.

As for punctuation, the word refers to something that occurs at intervals. It interrupts or disturbs the flow. So we might say 'the play was punctuated by applause'. However, the commonest use of the word refers to the small punctuation marks which interrupt the flow of words on a page. They make sentences and words easier to understand, reducing ambiguities.

Most children who read widely will naturally pick up the principles of punctuation. Quite young children sometimes ask what the dots and squiggles mean in books, and a quick explanation is usually sufficient. When they start creative writing, you can show them the conventions, if they have not grasped them.

You might ask, if grammar and punctuation are mostly intuitive, and learned in the toddler or early childhood years, what is the point of older children learning about parts of speech and grammar?

Firstly, it can help us in writing if we know how our language is correctly used. Conversation tends to be casual, but when we write letters, or job applications, or articles, it is important to know correct grammar and punctuation if we are not to appear ignorant. For instance, the phrase 'could have' is often pronounced 'could've' when we're talking. Unfortunately, people who do not understand the relevant grammar sometimes write or type it as 'could of', which sounds the same but is incorrect. Spell-checkers do not help with this kind of mistake. Nor do they help with the differences between 'your' and 'you're' or 'its' and 'it's'.

Secondly, if you learn a foreign language when you are a teenager or adult, you will discover that the grammar is likely to work differently from English grammar. If you learn a second language as a small child, you will understand this intuitively, as if it were your first language. But by the time we get to the age of around eight or nine, our brains have become somewhat hard-wired as far as language goes, and it is more difficult to learn a new one. So we have to learn how the grammatical structure of the new language works. Unless we understand at least the basics of English grammar first, that can be extremely difficult. Different languages sometimes use different punctuation marks, too.

Thirdly, in my opinion it can be interesting to study grammar, so long as you do not treat it as a chore. But I am a writer. Not everybody finds grammar to be of interest.

If your young children ask about punctuation marks or parts of speech, you could try making word cards of different colours, or highlighting phrases on paper with different coloured pens for different parts of speech. You could discuss the meanings of words when reading books together, or you could bring up a particular word you have heard, and wonder aloud what part of speech it is. There are no definitive answers in some complex cases.

If you repeat this kind of thing at random, or when your children ask about words, grammar will not seem like a tedious thing to study. Instead it may turn into a fascinating puzzle to solve. However, not everyone will find it interesting. As with any part of home education, there is no point in pushing something that leads to frustration or boredom. But if your child finds grammar intriguing, it can be a useful start to a study of linguistics, modern languages or classics. It can also help to lay a foundation for skills in categorising and logical thinking.

CHAPTER NINE
Other Subjects

Science

Science was the topic which was, to our family, the most daunting when we first considered home education. With memories of well-equipped laboratories, Bunsen burners, fume cupboards, high quality microscopes and an array of expensive chemicals, I could not imagine how parents at home could begin to emulate any of this.

The word 'science' means 'knowledge'. It is the study of the world around us. In essence, it's that simple, no matter how complex it seems when we wonder how to help our children to understand it.

There are three main branches of science: Biology looks at living things; chemistry looks at the elements and how they combine; physics looks at forces and the rules which the universe obeys. Each of these has many categories or subdivisions, such as botany, biochemistry, nuclear physics, and many more. But the start of all science is a questioning mind, and the attempt to make sense of who we are, and what our world is like.

A young child is usually an eager scientist. Your toddler may be full of questions about why birds fly, why the microwave makes things hot, or why the stars only come out at night. Some children ask endless questions of this kind which often leave the parent in despair, unable to answer even half of them. It can be all too easy to ask children to stop, or to give an offhand answer that does not really address their innate curiosity. But if we want our children to become thinkers and scientists, it is important to help them learn and understand these issues at the point when they are eager to do so.

That is not to say that we should launch into a lecture on quantum mechanics to a toddler. Sometimes a young child's question does not need a full explanation. This is why it is so important for parents to listen properly, so they understand what the child really means by a question. 'Why?' can happen after a child has puzzled about how or why something happens, but it might also be due to something that occurs to the child briefly, and which only needs a quick explanation.

Sometimes 'Why?' really means, 'I want to know more about this topic'. If you cannot answer a question to the child's satisfaction, a trip to the library to find a relevant book or a search online can show that you are taking his question seriously. This can lead to some positive educational moments for the adult, as well as for the child.

Some publishers have produced an excellent selection of science books for all ages. If your child regularly asks questions that fall in the science category, it is worthwhile spending some time browsing a large bookshop to find books at the right age and interest level. Styles vary and different children like different approaches.

Not every child asks, 'Why?', however. Some young children are less inclined to ask scientific questions.

If you feel the need to stimulate their interest in the subject, you can do so as part of ordinary conversation. Perhaps when you are out for a walk together you could talk about the seasons. I used to like pointing out buds and blossom on trees in the springtime. We would watch for leaves changing colour in Autumn, observe bare branches in winter. You could plant some seeds and watch their growth over several months. Even if you have no scientific background or interest yourself, you can help your children to be in awe of the wonder of nature and to understand that, by observation, we can learn what to expect in many situations.

You can also observe — and, if relevant, explain — scientific principles when your children are playing. If they notice different colours or sizes, they are learning simple analysis. If they sort blocks by colour, or cars by size, they are grasping the concept of categorisation. When your children play with toy trains or construction toys, you can show them how to make a simple lever, or a pulley. They will see principles such as the law of gravity in practice when they drop things, or when a toy car runs down a slope. When they push things on different surfaces, they are observing friction. As they grow older, your children will probably discover different and more efficient ways to build walls or tracks.

Thinking like a scientist involves coming up with suggestions, and then testing out ideas (experimenting) to see if they hold true. If not, a scientist re-formulates the initial suggestion (or hypothesis) and re-tests. This is a valuable principle to teach children from the time they can sit up and try things out for themselves. You can help them to think along these lines by posing theoretical questions: Will the water in this cup fit into that jar? Will the seeds grow if we don't give them any water? What will happen if we leave the chocolate in the sun?

Rather than telling your children what to expect, encourage them to guess, and then to observe and talk about what happens when they try it out. You can demonstrate the principle of a 'control' in an experiment by putting one piece of chocolate in the sun and one in the shade, to contrast how fast they melt. 'Let's see what happens!' should be at the heart of modern science, not: 'Do this and you will find that a specific result occurs'.

Primary school science, at its best, encourages children to be aware of the world around them, and to ask questions. It helps them to understand the concepts of fair testing and controlled experiments, and ways to note the results. It also helps them to observe patterns, and to be prepared for more formal scientific enquiry and investigation in later years.

Unfortunately, in a classroom environment it is difficult to teach science in a way which is inspiring to thirty children at the same time. What is obvious to one child may be new and exciting to another of the same age. If a child has played with simple electronic circuits at home, the building of a buzzer in school is going to seem like rather a waste of an afternoon. To another child it may be the highlight of the term. As with other topics, scientific home education can be targetted to each individual child.

Sometimes it can be interesting to show a child what happens under certain circumstances. Making a volcano by putting bicarbonate of soda into a plastic bottle and then pouring in vinegar mixed with red food colouring makes a dramatic and messy demonstration. It is best to do this outside, or in the kitchen sink. But note that this is not an experiment as such, unless you have discussed in advance what your child thinks might happen, and the child has proposed a hypothesis.

Still, if you have done the classic volcano-in-a-bottle, your child might wonder if the same thing would happen with other substances. This could form the basis of some real experiments. Perhaps you could substitute lemon juice for vinegar, or flour for bicarbonate of soda. You may need to be prepared with explanations about acids and alkalis, depending on the age and interest of your child. Alternatively, you could follow this with some baking that involves different chemical reactions.

In many cases, home educating families have a relative or friend who is an expert in some branch of science. If, like me, you feel totally at a loss with scientific questions, and if your older children or teenagers are asking practical questions which you cannot answer, it is probably time to ask for some help. Perhaps you know a car mechanic who would be happy to have your child assist in his work, and explain the principles of engines. Perhaps you know someone who works with electricity, who could show your child how to change fuses and wire plugs.

You can also find 'kits' for electronics, chemistry and various motors and other gadgets. These can satisfy some children's innate curiosity, and can help them to understand the relevant principles within the boundaries of the equipment provided. For those who want to know the principles but are not so interested in a hands-on experience, there are many relevant videos online, demonstrating scientific principles and investigations.

I remember growing rather a pretty copper sulphate crystal at school, and separating the inks in marker pens, using blotting paper. But have I ever needed either of these skills in adult life? No. Nowadays much of the chemistry taught in secondary schools involves demonstrations by staff from the front of the class, or from experts on video, rather than having much practical component for students. This is partly for financial reasons, but primarily for the sake of safety.

If home educated teenagers are eager to follow a career that needs science qualifications, there are courses available. If necessary, enrol them in an outside course at a college or adult education class. Or use a comprehensive correspondence package. If they are unsure, or if finances do not permit, there are some excellent GCSE level books in all three main branches of science which can be used at any age. A motivated teenager will learn a great deal on their own by following up questions and researching online.

But if your teenagers have no interest in science, there is no need to worry about it. Whatever they need to know for general information will probably crop up in conversation or life anyway. And what if — aged 18 — your child suddenly feels a vocation to be a doctor? Then they will have the intrinsic motivation needed to learn all they need in a few months; if necessary, there are foundation courses at universities that can facilitate this.

Our experience

By the time my elder son was twelve, he was firmly committed to learning at home. I bought school-type text books that showed scientific experiments, and we tried to work through them. But he found them dull. He had a good chemistry set, so we worked slowly through the book that came with it, reading about acids and alkalis, producing gases, discussing theories of molecules and chemical formulae. My younger son found it fascinating.

But my older son was still bored. 'How do you KNOW it's produced those things?' he would ask. 'It all just looks like white powders.' He was not convinced. If the book said that a gas that 'popped' was hydrogen, and we produced a gas that 'popped', that led to more questions. Why, my son wanted to know, did hydrogen pop? How could we know that there weren't other gases that popped? How could we tell that hydrogen had a particular atomic weight and that its molecules were arranged in a certain fashion, when we couldn't see them?

Since he did not have any interest in following a career related to chemistry, we gave up on that.

Next we ordered an American biology course. We started to read it together, and it was fascinating. But there were so many words to learn: types of amoeba, ways they reproduced, descriptions of the number of cells. We wondered what the point was of knowing all these words. Neither of my sons was likely to be a microbiologist. We skipped those sections and moved on to the part about the larger animal kingdom, but still there seemed to be definition after definition. The experiments were slightly more interesting than those in the chemistry book, but didn't prove — or even show — anything that my sons did not already know.

We bought some physics and chemistry GCSE text books from the UK. They had cartoons and humour as well as such good explanations of complex phenomena that even I could understand, albeit slowly. They were quite enjoyable to read through. But STILL there was nothing new to my sons which they found relevant. Either it was so theoretical that it seemed pointless, or they felt that it was obvious.

Finally it hit me. They were already knowledgeable about science. They knew what they needed to know about the human body, and about nature. Knowing the Latin words for internal organs might have been useful if either of them wanted to study medicine, but not otherwise. Understanding molecular structure at a theoretical level may be interesting, but producing new chemicals (which we could only identify because the book told us how to) was pointless if it was not going to be relevant to them in later life.

On the other hand, my sons learned far more about electronics than I was ever taught at school, from helping and observing their father. They built a computer out of old parts. They played with an electronics kit and taught themselves many things which would never be covered in a school curriculum. Simply reading — from textbooks and from other resources — slowly increased their background understanding, and paved the way for them to understand the world better.

Humanities

If you have read this far in the book, you will have realised that my approach to home education was fairly laid-back. At the same time, I never quite let go of the idea of needing 'core' subjects. As described in the earlier chapters of this section, at various times we used either text books or a curriculum to cover some basic topics. Yet there is so much more to life than maths, English and science. An important group of subjects are often categorised as 'humanities' — these include both creative arts and topics such as history, geography and religious education (RE).

I did not enjoy history or geography when I was at school. I don't have a good memory for facts, nor am I particularly visual, and frankly I found geography dull. History, as it was taught then, was a series of apparently random forays into different periods or cultures. So we might study the French Revolution one term, and the Ancient Greeks the next. There were dates and names and politics which, at secondary level, we were supposed to understand. But I somehow missed out on the big picture of history. It was not until I was an adult and started to read historical fiction that I discovered an angle — the personal one — that worked for me.

History and geography are taught rather differently in schools nowadays. Geography is a study of other cultures and social differences, as well as geology and weather patterns. Primary school geography deals with environmental issues: seeing how land erodes, understanding the water cycle, learning to read maps, looking at ecological concerns. It also compares other countries and cultures with ones' own.

While home educators do not have to cover any specific topics, this kind of thing is usually considered to be part of a broad general knowledge. In most cases children will ask relevant questions when they are ready, or the subjects will arise naturally.

Geography

If you travel abroad, you will have an immediate sense of geography — study of the world — around you. It can be interesting to talk with your children about the differences you see, and also any similarities with your own culture. If you have friends or relatives who live abroad, you could get in contact with them. Ask questions about their lives, learn about recent developments in their countries. Maybe ask about the kinds of produce that are grown, or local customs. If you live somewhere which has people from many different cultures, you could get to know some of them and talk about different foods, styles of dress, and cultural expectations.

On a short visit to another region within your own country there are also likely to be opportunities to talk about how different people live, and what differences you might expect to find. That is not to say that you need to talk about educational topics all the time. But in the course of everyday discussion, issues of this sort may well arise as you visit small villages or large towns. Historical discussion may naturally arise when you look at museums or ancient ruins. Cultural issues can surface when you search in supermarkets for familiar produce.

Even if you rarely stir outside your own local environment, and have no friends abroad, you can encourage your children to have an interest in the wider world. There are some excellent television or online documentaries about other countries, and many useful resources you can buy, or borrow from your library. A globe is a wonderful resource to see an overview of the world. Some children find them fascinating and learn a great deal from them about other continents and the names of countries. Atlases are interesting to browse too, and often have general information about other countries and cultures.

Google Earth is an excellent resource for your computer or tablet, enabling you to explore most of the world from your own home. You can show your children places you have been, or countries they have heard of in books or on television. In some cases you can zoom in to see streets and houses, and perhaps talk about how different they are in other parts of the world.

You can help your children understand maps as soon as they start to read. If you point out your street on a local map, and other places of interest, then you may find your children following maps in the car when you drive anywhere, rather than continually asking when you will arrive. You can help them to understand the concepts of keys and scale, and give them appropriate maps to follow whenever you travel. While people tend to use phones or GPS devices in cars nowadays, a map or atlas is still a useful thing to be able to follow.

Board games like Risk or Ticket to Ride give a general big picture of world geography, albeit with inaccuracies. There are many online or computer games which give the player a chance to simulate different environments and explore what happens under different conditions. As children grow older, they will hear about earthquakes and war zones and tsunamis — as questions arise, make sure you help them find answers that satisfy them.

As for weather and the water cycle, we see those around us and questions are likely to arise in everyday life. Where does our tap water come from? Why does it sometimes taste strange? What happens when we filter water? What do those clouds mean...? If your children do not ask questions like this, try asking them what they think, to stimulate their curiosity.

Some home educating parents avoid this kind of thing, wanting every query to come from the child. But I cannot see any harm in pointing out something children might not have noticed, or asking a few leading questions. Just make sure you stop when they lose interest, and pitch it at the appropriate level without turning it into a lesson.

Teaching your children the skills to do their own geography research is more important than studying specific topics. As you talk about different cultures, it can be good to help them realise that there is no 'best' or 'worst' country or culture; they are all different, with positive and negative features. Moreover, some customs which seem strange to us are taken for granted elsewhere. The more your children mix with people from other cultures, and learn about the ways they live, the more likely they are to develop into broad-minded adults who can develop friendships with people from anywhere in the world.

History

History taught in schools inevitably covers a few slices of particular periods or cultures. No matter how well it is presented, some children are unable to perceive an overview of history, or to see how one period relates to another. At home, not tied to specific curriculum topics, your children can learn about any period or culture that interests them, and gradually build up an awareness of the big picture of the past.

If you are not confident about history yourself, you could start by researching your local area and its history with your children. You could visit the local library for information, and explore some old houses, churches and museums. If you have an elderly friend or relative who has lived through exciting times, you could encourage your children to think of questions they would like to ask about the past. Perhaps you could cook the kind of food that was eaten in the War, and help your children imagine, role-play or write stories about some of the scenes from the past.

For younger children, you could think about a specific topic such as food, clothes, or homes and find out together how different people have lived over the centuries. If they are interested, you can help them to understand about the past, to see what changes have come over recent decades, and to discuss the advantages and disadvantages of modern life. You will find a wide variety of books in your bookshop and library.

An excellent series of books is the 'Horrible History'

series, written for children of around 8–12 with a humorous — but accurate — view of history, including many of the unpleasant and gory parts. Reading these gives a good overview of the periods covered, and shows something of the life of children as well as adults. There are many titles in the series; if your children like them, they may learn a great deal about history from them. For those who prefer fiction, historical novels set in the appropriate period will help your children to get a feel for the subject. There are some excellent historical fiction books written for children which give the context of significant world events.

If your child is interested in history, and wants some structure to his education, you could suggest a project on a specific topic. He could then research the topic online and in books, and produce a booklet about it. This is useful in helping children to learn about checking sources, cross-referencing and other research skills as well as about the history topic itself.

At some point you may want to make a history timeline. One method of doing this is to choose a country or continent and chart their monarchs or main events over the years, spacing the time line appropriately. Alternatively, you could take the whole world and make a more general timeline. There are many websites which give the necessary information to print out relevant dates and facts, and you can encourage younger children to draw and write appropriate pieces.

Another option is to build a folder with one page about each time and culture, with key points of the periods. If done via computer, it can include diagrams and clips from online research. Enthusiastic children and teens can learn a great deal from this; but, again, don't try to persuade them to keep going when they lost interest.

Learning happens best when the student is motivated and enthusiastic, and children may return to projects they abandoned if they are free to study in the ways that best suit their personalities and interests.

Religious Education

Religious education is one of the most controversial subjects taught in school. Some countries have removed it from the curriculum entirely. In the UK it is still compulsory, and must cover a wide range of topics, including introductions to all the major world religions. Whatever your religious beliefs (or lack thereof), we live in multi-ethnic societies. If we want to understand those around us, we must be aware of their religions. If we hope to be ethnically aware, and able to communicate well with our neighbours, it is important to respect their views, and to teach our children to do so.

If you are a person of faith, or belong to a religious tradition, you will probably introduce this to your child from a young age. This is what we did. My husband and I both come from an Anglican Christian background. We brought up our sons as Christians in a mostly non-denominational and entirely un-fundamentalist way. We made a point of saying a prayer with them at night, when they were small, and giving thanks before a meal. Stories from the Bible made part of our regular reading, and our children attended toddler groups and playgroups that were linked with churches. We belonged to a church congregation that had several young families, and it was natural that our children attended Sunday School, holiday clubs, and other low-key Christian events.

When we lived in Birmingham, surrounded by people of different faiths, it was natural to explain, as the children grew older, that some people believed different things. While we explained what we believed, we felt that it was important for the boys to ask questions and, at times, express doubts. Whatever your faith, or even if you are an atheist or agnostic, make sure you talk about other faiths and beliefs without being derogatory or condescending.

There are no absolute proofs of the existence of God. Nor are there any proofs that God does not exist. As a home educator, you have the opportunity to explain the big picture and to enable your children to see why different faiths developed. As with other historical figures, the Internet makes it easy to research people such as Jesus, Mohammed, Moses, Buddha and so on. Perhaps you can visit local places of worship and ask questions. You may find a priest or Imam willing to explain their beliefs, and maybe offer informational leaflets.

If you are uncertain about what other faiths believe, there are many books and websites that look objectively at world religions, showing similarities and differences. Some of them explain the variety of beliefs related to topics such as life after death. If you raise your children to be respectful towards those with differing faiths, you will help them to become globally aware. This should enable them to chat intelligently to anyone they meet or work with in future.

Other subjects

When we started home education, I knew I could manage the academic subjects, at least at primary level. My bigger concern was for what might loosely be termed the creative arts. These include drawing, painting, crafts, singing, music in general, and drama. I was less worried about cooking, knitting or sewing, as I knew I could teach those, should my sons be interested. But my art-related skills and knowledge were almost non-existent, and the extent of my drama career was being a tree in a school play.

I went to a highly academic girls' school. I liked several subjects, particularly maths and classics. Yet the things I still use are skills that I learned in home economics: cooking and nutrition. I am not a musician, but I like being able to understand rhythms, and having the ability to read at least simple music. I also benefited from being introduced to styles of music I might not otherwise have heard.

If parents are artistically or musically inclined, then this part of home education should not cause any difficulties. But to me, encouraging my children's creativity seemed to be far more of a challenge than helping them understand literature, or learn new maths concepts.

This section discusses, briefly, some more of the non-core subjects that might interest your children. It is more personal than some of the others in that it explains in some detail what we did; as always, I share them as examples rather than suggestions. Many families manage this far better than we did and your experience is likely to be entirely different from ours.

Music

You can introduce children to music from birth — or before birth, if you listen to music regularly. Some babies in the womb react by kicking or moving to strong rhythms, and some appear to be soothed, after birth, by music that has been played during pregnancy. Some classical music has been shown to calm fractious babies and toddlers, and to help children relax and learn more while studying.

If you like singing, then you probably sing with your

children in the car, or around the house; if not, you can find music of almost any kind online to play to your children, and they are likely to sing or dance naturally if it appeals to them. If you belong to a toddler group, your children will hear singing there.

Once your children are beyond the toddler stage, you might find a local music shop which encourages children to try out various keyboards or other instruments. If they like banging pans, a child's percussion set or even a simple drum kit can make a useful addition to the house, if you do not mind the noise.

Look out for local choirs for children, or musical appreciation days, and try to take them to local concerts or productions (sometimes done by schools) of musicals. It should become clear at a fairly young age if a child is likely to be musical; if so, and if this is not your forte, you may want to look at outside music lessons.

It was evident before we moved to Cyprus that both our sons were musical. In the UK, they sang in an excellent children's choir which regularly performed in public. They sang in their school choir too. Our older son, at eleven, played three different recorders and was part of his school recorder consort. He had reached Grade 3 level in clarinet, as well as being part of the school wind band. He had taken private piano lessons for a couple of years too. Our younger son, at nine, had done a year of recorder, and taken a year of piano lessons, and was eager to learn the guitar.

So one of my biggest reservations about home education was the lack of free or inexpensive music tuition. One of our new colleagues in Cyprus had offered to give both our sons piano lessons, at no cost. But despite this generous offer I had no idea how to offer the breadth of musical experience that they had in their UK primary school.

Writing this twenty years later, I still feel that this was the most difficult part of home education for us. We did manage to find a clarinet teacher for our older son, although it was not easy. After a couple of years he was able to play in the town marching band, which was a good experience. Occasionally both sons were able to play recorders with enthusiastic and talented friends, but these friends lived in another town and we did not see them very often.

Our younger son joined a Greek choir for some months, although all the other members were adults. Both of them took part in inter-church carol concerts. They joined the church music group, and, in their teens, one son was part of the youth group band. They sometimes had 'jamming' sessions with home educating friends, or when we had musical visitors staying. We had to ensure we took advantage of as many opportunities as possible, as they did not happen very often.

Still, although our older son gave up piano lessons after a couple of years in Cyprus, he started drum lessons when he was fifteen, with a local teacher. He also managed to find a more advanced clarinet teacher in another town; he even organised his own transport with friends or via buses. Our younger son continued piano lessons; he also took guitar lessons from a friend for a year, then decided he would prefer to teach himself as his motivation was to accompany himself or others singing rather than to play classical pieces.

On the negative side, we did not study any music appreciation, or the history of music. I don't tend to listen to music, and we don't sing at home. But, looking back, I realise now that the boys' passion for music pushed us into finding suitable teachers, and — when necessary — funding them. Finances were tight, but music was an important priority. As they grew older, they took the initiative in finding their own teachers and people to make music with.

Since leaving home our older son has had little time to make music, although he still sometimes plays drums or other instruments as part of a group. Our younger son, on the other hand, is now employed as a music teacher. So despite our personal inability to educate them musically, they do not seem to have missed out.

Art and craft

Young children seem naturally drawn to arts and crafts; all parents need to do, in the early years, is to supply paper, cardboard, sticky tape (lots of it!), scissors, and crayons or paints. Many children like to colour ready-drawn pictures, and there are many available, mostly inexpensive, or you can print pictures to colour downloaded from your computer.

Encourage all efforts. Do not worry be concerned about whether children colour 'within the lines', or use appropriate colours. If your child colours a horse green and its rider with pink hair and a blue face, that is a form of creative expression. If your child draws what looks like a scribble and announces that it is a portrait of Grandpa, then the best thing to do is to put it up on the fridge or some other suitable place for everyone to see. You could add a label underneath (if your child would like you to write one) so that visitors know what is being represented.

If your children show an interest in art, there are many more advanced supplies that you can find at stationery shops. There are some excellent books showing techniques with charcoal, pastels, water painting and oils or acrylics, and it is worth getting hold of these — or watching suitable videos online — if your child is keen to learn.

Art galleries can provide inspiration for further projects. Even if you do not have a local one, you can often find them online. There may be links to information about artists or artistic techniques. Some of them have sculptures or other forms of art too.

I know even less about art than I do about music, but I managed to make simple items out of old boxes with my sons, and we had fun with playdough and plasticine, creating miniature animals or food items. Small children are not critical of adults' attempts, and older ones who have some skill at craft seem to learn without direct teaching, so long as they have plenty of opportunity.

Our older son was a natural artist from the time he first held a pencil and drew a line on a piece of paper in his high chair. Our younger son was less interested in art. I used to leave plenty of paper and craft supplies around when they were small; they would experiment with drawing, and cutting, and sticking, and so on. As they grew older, they played with paper crafts or origami, and developed the ability to colour and build models.

Lego was a large part of their life; we collected many sets, mostly given by generous relatives at birthdays and Christmas. They would initially build the models as given in the instructions, and play with them for a few days; then they would adapt them, and re-build them with other pieces, and so create their own extensive imaginary worlds.

Shortly after we started home education, we found a teacher offering Saturday morning art sessions at minimal cost. I hoped that this would encourage them both as well as giving some expert artistic input. Our younger son soon lost interest, but our older son did some excellent still life drawings and paintings in the two or three years in which he attended these sessions.

As a teenager, our older son also developed skill in computer graphics, using a variety of different software that was available at the time. This was all self-taught. We subscribed, for a while, to a computer arts magazine from the UK, and he joined some online forums. He created images for our Christmas cards for several years, and soon moved into the realm of 3D computer graphics, with the application 'Blender', one which he still uses as an adult.

Drama

Dramatic expression can be used while reading aloud, or playing imaginary games with young children. But drama as taught in schools is hard to replicate at home. When we met our home educating friends, there were some attempts by the older children to produce plays, from time to time, and our sons enjoyed doing so. But there was no real direction, and they often gave up and did other activities instead.

Our older son took part in one or two small plays or skits at our church and in the youth group, but did not show much interest in drama in general until he was fifteen. At that point, he became very keen. He joined the teenage group of a local theatre company, where he flourished. He took part in a competition production within a few months of joining, playing a key role. A couple of years later, he was able to join with the leaders of the company in some professional productions. This was only possible because he was home educated: he was not caught up in exams and homework like most of the others in his group.

Our younger son was not interested in being on stage as an actor, but helped sometimes with the sound and lighting. My husband became involved with the company in an advisory role related to lighting and sound production. Both our sons learned a great deal from him, as they helped him to instal, set up and run sound and/or lights.

I felt bad, for a while, that they missed out on the fun of creating and producing school assemblies; of reading plays in English classes, of annual productions put on in schools. Yet I never much enjoyed those when I was at school. And despite this lack, our older son was able to take UK drama exams through the theatre company. Since leaving home, he has sometimes taken part in theatre or video productions.

Once again, our sons' interests guided them into places where they could learn and try out new skills, even though we could not offer them ourselves at home.

Languages

Learning another language is compulsory in British schools, and is often very useful later in life. The ideal way for a young child to learn another language is by immersion, or by hearing it exclusively from a native speaker. So if a close friend or relative is a fluent speaker of a language other than English, then the best thing to do is for that person to speak only to your children in that language.

When parents do this from birth — one speaking French and the other English, for instance — children naturally grow up bilingual. They are likely to favour one language for speaking amongst themselves — usually the language of the mother, or that of the country where they are living — but will understand and have a good accent for the other language too.

If you know of people who have other native languages, and they are willing to use them with your children, then they may grow up understanding three,

Other Subjects

four or even more languages. This is normal in some countries of the world. I have met children of just four or five years old who communicate regularly in at least four different languages which they have heard around them since babyhood.

Unfortunately, this is not possible for many of us. So if you cannot expose your child to another language in this way, you will have to decide whether or not it is a priority for you to help them learn another language, and which one to study. That may be determined by location, or by places you travel to or people you know. Or you could choose a language at random.

There are many online resources now for teaching almost any language of the world. When we started home education, we decided to learn Greek as we were living in a Greek-speaking country. We borrowed an audio course, but it was really intended for adults. We tried an online course, but that, too, was not suitable for children and progressed rather more rapidly than we were ready for. Still, we picked up some basics which were useful.

We then tried books; one of my sons took Greek lessons for a while. Both of them picked up some everyday Greek from the various groups they went to, but neither became fully fluent. Too many people in Cyprus speak excellent English and we found it surprisingly hard to learn Greek when nobody would use it with us.

My younger son decided to study French for a few years, and we tried various courses. He learned some basic grammar and vocabulary, but did not take it very far.

Now as adults both sons have started learning other languages with online courses, as they have needed them. Neither French nor Greek has proved to be of much use, but they both have a reasonable understanding of how other languages work, meaning that they do not struggle with concepts alien to English such as 'gender' in objects, or different verb endings.

CHAPTER TEN
Exams and University

GCSEs and A-levels

Home educators are often asked how their children can get to university or find employment if they do not take school exams. If your child is young, it is best to give a vague answer rather than being defensive (or replying at length). Exams can be studied for at home. Some students go to school or sixth form college in their teens. Some prefer not to go the academic route through university anyway.

When you are discussing something at least ten years in the future, there is little point going into detail. The system will probably have changed — as it does regularly — by the time your child is at the stage of considering a future career. So if your children are still young, this section is not relevant to you. It may no longer be correct by the time your child reaches the age of thinking about exams or university.

However, if you have older children who are interested in further education, it is a good idea to look at what they need to do in preparation for the course or courses they are thinking about. The UCAS (Universities and Collages Admissions Service) site can be browsed by anyone, and will give you an idea of what kinds of prerequisites are necessary for different courses. These varies from university to university, and it may be possible to get in touch with specific universities directly to ask what options there are for home educators.

Typically, university courses require for A-level exams or equivalent in the topic to be studied. In order to take A-levels, it is usually necessary to have taken the relevant GCSEs. There are other routes to university — discussed in the next section — but many home educators do take these standard exams. This page explains what they are, why it might be worth taking them, and some of the options for doing so.

GCSE stands for General Certificate of Secondary Education. GCSEs are exams taken by UK school students at around the age of fifteen or sixteen, in different subjects. There is a core set of exams taken by the majority: this usually includes at least maths, English, a foreign language and a science. Some students take just two or three GCSEs, others take eight or nine, with some schools offering advanced students ten or more different GCSEs.

While GCSEs are not compulsory, they are standard in most UK schools. This means that many employers expect a minimum number of them, often asking for reasonable grades in maths and English. The reason is that GCSEs are an easy way to demonstrate a measure of competence, for instance in literacy and basic numeracy. That does not mean that home educators have to take them. But if they don't, they may need to find ways around the general requirements, or other ways of proving satisfactory levels of learning and understanding.

A-levels are advanced exams, usually taken by students of seventeen or eighteen, after two further years of study in a school 'sixth form' (years 12 and 13) or a specific sixth form college. Typically three or four A-levels are taken by each student, enabling them to study at a deeper and more advanced level than is possible with GCSEs.

A sixth-form college may also offer some GCSEs, either as extra subjects, or as re-takes for students who did not get the grades they needed. When taking GCSEs at schools or sixth-form colleges, there is no cost to the students. Most course materials, the marking of any coursework and the cost of the exam itself are usually all borne by the school or college. One perceived disadvantage of home education is that when students want to take these exams, all costs must be covered by the families.

Nevertheless, they are useful qualifications for university or job applications. GCSE courses — which typically take about two years per subject in schools — can be studied outside a formal environment, and can be started at any age. Some home educated students begin quite young, following courses that they are particularly interested in. It is possible to take one or two GCSEs per year based on abilities and interests. This can help to spread the cost, and also allows for more focussed studying rather than trying to do several different courses at the same time.

Other home educated students wait until they are sixteen or seventeen before embarking on any formal study. They then enrol at a sixth-form college to take GCSE subjects or A-levels appropriate to their future careers. Until they are beyond the compulsory education age, they can do so without significant cost. Some colleges will admit younger students, but may charge them more. Others may not admit younger students at all, particularly if the courses are popular and likely to be over-subscribed.

It is also possible to study the course material at home, by oneself. It is then necessary to find an official local venue for taking the exams and to register as an external candidate. Not all schools or other exam centres allow external candidates, and those that do will ask for a fee for each exam.

Another possibility is to use a correspondence course. There are many organisations which offer tuition for distance learning and materials online, although they can be pricey. If you follow this path, please read the terms and conditions carefully before making any financial commitment. The styles and resources supplied vary quite a bit, and not every course is necessarily suitable for your child. Still, if money is not a problem, these courses can be an excellent way for students to study material at a level beyond the parents' knowledge, and to gain suitable qualifications. Again, a local exam centre will have to be found for the exams.

When there is no money for this kind of thing, and a teenager is keen to take exams around the same time as his schooled contemporaries, it may be worth looking at local secondary schools. Year 10 is when most GCSE courses begin, with exams taken at the end of Year 11. Depending on your reasons for choosing home education originally, this can be a good solution: many students are educated at home until they are fourteen or fifteen, and then enrol at a suitable local school at the start of Year 10. Those I have heard about found it easy to settle in and make friends, and had no difficulty with the work, even if they were autonomously educated up to that point.

However, if your child had problems with bullying, or did not find it easy to work in a classroom for any reason, they may prefer to study for GCSEs or A-levels at home. If so, it is important to note that each exam board may have specific requirements for each year. General GCSE or A-level books or revision guides which you can find in the shops give an overview of what is likely to be studied, but you will need to see past papers, and in many cases use specific books that are required by your chosen board. This is particularly important in subjects such as English Literature, where different authors or novels are studied each year.

GCSEs taken in schools sometimes include a significant amount of graded coursework. This consists of projects, essays or other assignments done during the year which count towards the final grade. This is ideal for students who find exams stressful: it can be encouraging to know that a percentage of the grade is already achieved. However it can be more difficult for home educated students to manage coursework, because it must be marked by an independent person. The IGCSE (International GCSE) exams have no graded coursework, relying entirely on exams. This suits some students well, and may be worth investigating.

It is important to remember that GCSEs and/or A-levels should be taken because the child wants to do them, perhaps because they will be useful for future education or career options. Neither of my sons took any, and it did not affect their careers in any way.

Note, too, that some A-level courses can be taken directly without the relevant GCSE, and some vocational courses or careers do not require paper qualifications. There is little point putting a home educated child under pressure to take courses or exams unless it is their own decision.

Applying for university

If your student takes A-levels, at sixth form college or elsewhere, then applying to university is usually straightforward. Indeed, if a teenager knows for certain that he or she wants further education, the benefits of a good sixth form college may well outweigh any disadvantages. A-levels can be studied at home, too, either through books or a correspondence course.

However, there are home educated students in the UK and elsewhere who have gone to university without A-levels. My younger son is one of them (our story is told, in some detail, in the final chapters). In some cases students have no formal qualifications at all. Universities may be interested in well-rounded students who can demonstrate a passion for their chosen subject. When a teenager is not in school, there is time for deeper study or relevant experiences that are not always possible for students at school or sixth-form college. Thus (depending on what course is being applied for) relevant work experience, or evidence of extensive personal studying, or a good portfolio may be of great value when applying to university.

Another option is to choose a foundation degree. These are particularly suitable for those who are practical as well as academic. They may also be relevant to those want to study degree-level courses such as architecture or business, where there are unlikely to be relevant A-levels. Foundation courses do not have any entry requirements, and generally combine work experience with academic learning. In many cases, after achieving a foundation degree, a student can opt to do further study which leads to a standard honours degree.

Applications to British universities have to be made through the UCAS website, usually in the year before the student hopes to start studying at the university. UCAS has a system of 'points' which many universities follow. Typically, three A-levels would be accepted for many courses, but – depending on the course – specific ones may be required, and/or particular grades. Qualifications from other sources such as music or ballet exams, may also be acceptable, depending on the course being studied. You can find full details of how points are calculated on the 'tariff' page of the UCAS site.

Thus it is important for any home educated student considering further education to start looking, by the mid-teenage years, at what different universities may require for their chosen field. A student wanting to study medicine, for instance, will find it easiest to take three A-levels, including biology and chemistry, although it may be possible to take a foundation degree in science instead. A student wanting to study art should be building up a portfolio of styles, and perhaps aiming to take at least a GCSE in Art.

The UCAS application form also asks the student to describe their interests, their achievements, and why they are applying. The personal statement is probably the most important part of the application, so students should make sure they spend plenty of time on this. Preparing it in a word processor is best rather than typing it in directly. It should then be checked by a parent or other suitable adult to ensure that it includes relevant information and is well structured without unnecessary padding.

A referee is also needed for UCAS applications. Note that a parent will not be able to provide a student's official reference. If they have done paid or voluntary work, or studied for qualifications such as music or drama exams, there may be a teacher or employer who can provide an academic or character reference. A minister or youth group leader may be another possibility, or – if correspondence courses have been taken – a tutor. It should ideally be someone who is aware of the student's academic potential and work ethic, and also how well he is likely to interact with other students.

Home educated teenagers usually enjoy not just the freedom and focus of home education, but being able to work at home, at their own pace. Depending on their personalities and learning styles, they may prefer studying without the interaction of other students. There are also many home educated students who have found jobs or voluntary work, but want to do some part-time formal studying.

In these cases, online degree courses may be a better option than studying at a bricks-and-mortar university. The Open University is ideal in such circumstances, if finances permit. It provides some excellent courses and is highly flexible, with no entry requirements. Moreover, some of the shorter or more basic Open University courses, once passed, may themselves count towards the qualifications necessary for a traditional university application.

As well as the Open University itself, there are other universities which offer 'open' courses that can be studied at home. These vary from year to year, so the best place to find out what is available is to search online. Depending on where you live, and the age of your student, there may be some funding or student loans available; it's worth consulting the Student Finance website to find out what needs to be done to take advantage of this, if relevant.

Although university can seem like the default option to many people who have grown up in academic environments, people are beginning to question how useful a degree is in the 21st century. For one thing, the fees have risen sharply in recent years and a hefty student loan is an unpleasant burden to start working life with. The number of unemployed graduates in their twenties has also increased. Older people are working for longer as the retirement age has increased, and employers often want relevant experience rather than academic qualifications.

Some careers – medicine, law, teaching, etc – require degrees, and jobs at the end are not usually too hard to find. Students who feel a sense of vocation in academic fields such as these will almost certainly find a way to get to university, and perhaps some of the funding too.

However, if a career does not need a degree, then home educated students, without the limitations of a classroom timetable, may be able to volunteer or do part-time work in their chosen field before they finish their compulsory education years. In some cases, this can lead to a full-time job once they are the right age. An 18-year-old with paid employment, even on minimum wage, will be a great deal better off financially by his mid-twenties than a graduate saddled with a large student debt and no guaranteed job.

Many people nowadays choose to delay university entrance until they can support themselves financially. Then they either study part-time courses while still working, or take a sabbatical to study full-time after saving towards the necessary fees. Note, too, that 'mature' students – those over the age of 25 – may have fewer entrance requirements than those of 18. In addition, they are likely to be more motivated than some school-leavers, some of whom start university courses merely because they can't think of anything else to do.

Epilogue
Our Home Education Journey

The primary years

Our sons were born towards the end of the 1980s, before the introduction of the UK National Curriculum. Children were expected to start school the September before their 5th birthdays in our district; my sons both had Autumn birthdays, so were due to start just before they turned five.

In those days there were mother-and-toddler groups in church halls, and playgroups where parents could volunteer as committee members or helpers. There were state-run half-time nursery schools too. So many people recommended nursery as a precursor to school that we applied for a place, and moved our older son there when he was almost four, although in retrospect I think he might have been happier to stay at the playgroups for another year. We had no idea that home education was possible, and were caught up in the mindset of children needing to be 'socialised' at a young age.

1991-1992: Reception (UK)

We put our son's name down for a couple of good local state schools equidistant from our house, and visited them both. We chatted with parents and children who attended them, and on balance liked the smaller Church of England school better. Our son was offered places at each of these schools, and we accepted the C of E one. He started about a month before his fifth birthday. There were a few miserable days and some stresses. We were assured that most children had a hard time starting school, and there were bound to be a few tears.

Why didn't I query this at the time? I have no idea. I still believe it was a good school, and that the staff did all they could to ease the children in gradually to their new environment. The Reception class teacher was enthusiastic and caring. She quickly got to know all the children's personalities; she understood different learning styles. She recognised that each child learned to read in different ways and at different rates. She was also excellent at communicating with parents.

However, the days were tiring, the children did not always get along with each other, and the work was not always interesting. Our son asked for a globe for his fifth birthday. He was thrilled when he opened the one we bought him, and I loved seeing the delight and amazement in his eyes as he looked at the different countries, was surprised at how small the UK looked, and remarked on the vastness of the oceans. On the way to school that morning he asked me questions about why people in Australia didn't fall off, and how the world revolved. My understanding of gravity was basic so I suggested he could ask his teacher. He sighed, and said that there was no time to ask questions in school — they had to learn lessons. This was in the days when the Reception class was mostly informal, with plenty of play and scope for individual learning — or so I had thought.

Was this school, excellent though it was in many respects, the right place for our sensitive, creative son who found it so deeply stressful at times? I don't know. We cannot go back in time, and I still think it was the most suitable school in the neighbourhood. After the first few weeks he was mostly happy enough there, and quickly made some friends. He was beginning to read by the end of the year, and was considered to be good at both maths and art.

Meanwhile our younger son, who was three, decided that he wanted to read too. He was thoroughly enjoying the two playgroups he belonged to, but in the afternoons would find his brother's reading books, and work through them. He asked me to run my finger under the words whenever I read to him, and he wanted to know what words said on signs that we saw when out and about. He played extensively with magnetic fridge letters too, making both real and imaginary words.

1992-1994: First and Second Grade (USA)

In the summer of 1992 we moved to the United States for two years. We assumed that the local schools would be comparable with those in the UK. However, we were surprised to find that school starting ages were higher in Colorado. Our first son, we were told, should go into half-time Kindergarten. When the local school Principal realised that he could read and write simple sentences, he was surprised. He didn't think it was possible for a not-quite-six-year-old child to read. We didn't tell him that our younger son, who was not quite four, could also read at the same level.

So the Principal said that, if we really wanted him to, our son could go into First Grade. School in Colorado was not a good experience. Our son went from being mostly happy to being depressed and angry. His teacher was rigid in her methods: not unpleasant, but unwilling to make any concessions. Some of the children, up to two years older, were decidedly unfriendly. The work was tedious; at one point the teacher said our son probably had ADHD, something I had not heard of at the time. A third of her class, she told us, were on drugs to help them concentrate. Our son told us that he stared out of the classroom window rather than working because he was bored. He knew that if he finished his worksheet quickly he would not be given anything interesting or more challenging to do: he would be given another worksheet that was even more boring.

We first heard of 'homeschooling' when we lived in the US. We had some friends who educated their children this way, but we didn't see how we could afford it. They used an expensive curriculum and didn't tell us that there were other, cheaper methods. Perhaps they didn't know. We were struggling financially with a poor exchange rate and much higher medical insurance costs than we had expected, so we had nothing extra. My husband was unimpressed with the idea of homeschooling anyway. From his perspective, school was meant to teach children to be bored and to work hard for other people. He did not enjoy his own school experience, but felt it was necessary to survive adult life. (Thankfully this attitude changed a few years later).

So our older son went through First and Second Grade in Colorado, growing more and more fed up and unhappy. Years later, he said that he learned two things while he was there: how to spell Mississippi and the names of the body parts of a spider.

We cannot change history, but one of my biggest regrets is that we did not pull him out of school as soon as we knew that we could legally do so. He would have learned more and been a great deal happier even if he had sat and watched television all day.

I am now thankful that our younger son, despite reading fluently by the time he was five, was not old enough to go to Kindergarten in Colorado. He was a sociable child, and I was quite upset when I realised that there was no flexibility in the minimum age requirements. Worse, there were no free nursery schools or even inexpensive playgroups. But we bought some workbooks (at his request) and read lots of books together, and he taught himself to be computer literate in those two years.

1994-1997: school for both (UK)

We returned to the UK after two years in the US, and places were found for both our sons at the same small local C of E school. They settled in quickly, and our older son started coming out of school smiling, telling us with enthusiasm what they had done: art projects, maths, creative writing, and — best of all — learning to play the recorder. It was only then that I realised how damaging the Colorado school had been to our sensitive son. Now he felt at home again. His confidence was rebuilt, and if he finished work in class quickly, he was given something more challenging or interesting to do.

While chatting with a friend, during this period, the topic of homeschooling came up. I asked if it was legal in the UK, and she assured me that it was (which is true) but that one had to be a qualified teacher (which is not true). I still thought of it as a last resort rather than a positive option and saw no reason to look into it. I started volunteering in the boys' school, at first for one morning per week, eventually for two full days. Had we stayed, I might have trained as a classroom assistant.

In the summer of 1997 we started looking at potential secondary schools for our first son. There were selective grammar schools, which would probably have suited him well. But they were very popular and he was not the kind of child to do well in pressurised exams. We looked at three local state schools too. One was huge, and impersonal, and shocked us by displaying proudly a banner stating that 'only' 25% of their students had been badly bullied in the past year. Another school was small and friendly, but the academic quality was poor, the labs badly equipped, the music standard low. The third seemed like a good school, and many of our son's friends would go there. It had the advantage of being very close to our house, but the disadvantage of being a school for boys only. My husband felt strongly that mixed schools were far superior, particularly for boys.

1997-1998: home education (Cyprus)

Thankfully we did not have to make a decision about secondary schools. At the end of October 1997 (when our older son had just started Year Six, and our younger son was in Year Four) we moved to Cyprus. We had corresponded with colleagues, as I had been concerned about the boys' education. The state schools in Cyprus, we learned, were all Greek-speaking. There were several private English primary schools on the island, including one in the town we were going to live in, and one on the army base twenty miles away. They were expensive and, once again, our finances were tight, although relatives had offered to help if we needed to pay for the boys' education.

To my surprise, our older son asked if we could 'homeschool' for the first few months. He said he did NOT want to go straight into a school as he had done in Colorado. He wanted a chance to settle in, and to find out what the schools were like, before making any long-term decisions. It made sense, particularly as we were going to arrive after the start of a school year. We talked to their primary school staff in the UK, a little tentatively. To our surprise, they all thought it would be a good idea. They added that moving abroad was an educational experience in itself, and that the boys would probably benefit significantly from a year off school.

It helped (in the school staff's eyes, anyway) that both boys were well advanced, by this stage, in reading and writing. Both were in the top groups in their classes for maths, too. Both were more experienced than their teachers in IT. I knew from my time volunteering in the classrooms that I could keep up with other subjects, at least at primary level. On the advice of the staff we ordered some maths books, and were given a scheme of work that told us what their age groups would be doing at the school through the year for each subject. We assumed that we would be returning to the UK after a couple of years, so I wanted to ensure they covered the majority of what they would have been doing in school.

When we arrived, we visited the English-speaking primary schools nearby, still unsure about our decision. Our younger son had loved school and did not like the thought of home education at all. However, the local private school was rigid and old-fashioned, following an American maths curriculum that did nothing much other than arithmetic, with endless drill. The Head at the time insisted that, at just nine, he could not possibly want to read anything beyond the limited shelf of books intended for his age group. The school offered no music, no art, and very little PE.

So we embarked on home education for the rest of that academic year. We started by planning a structured timetable, but soon found that we were being over-ambitious. Gradually our style became more relaxed and eclectic over the year as we all went through the de-schooling process. I discovered that the boys could cover a term's worth of maths or English in an hour if they felt motivated. If they were not motivated, it was pointless to try.

In the spring of 1998, I mentioned that we should look at secondary schools. There were two English-speaking private ones near to where we lived, both considered to be good. To my surprise, our older son asked if we could continue home education as he was enjoying it so much.

I felt daunted. My knowledge of secondary level geography, science and history was minimal. My son pointed out that I had been to a good school. So if I had forgotten most of what I learned, what was the point?

By then, my husband had realised how much more fulfilled we all were with home education. And our younger son, who had a good friend in the local English-speaking primary school, heard such horror stories of teachers yelling and tedious homework that he said he would like to continue home education for a couple more years, too.

The secondary years

1998-2000: home education continued

In the summer of 1998 we ordered more resources, and I read as much as I could about education in the secondary years. With some apprehension and much discussion, we all committed to another two years of home education. Our younger son was pretty sure that he would want to go to secondary school when he was old enough, and I thought our older son would probably need to do so around the same time. I thought they would need to be able to take exams and gain qualifications for future careers or university.

During that period, we changed our style regularly. Our older son was usually self-motivated and creative; he learned things that interested him without any real structure. He would lie in bed at night, reading encyclopaedias. At random times he would ask questions about places or people he had heard about on the radio. He read magazines, and picked the brains of anyone he knew who was interested in something he wanted to know about.

From his point of view, unschooling or autonomous education was perfect. He wrote extensively, including starting a complex fantasy novel, though he did not complete it. He won a couple of prizes in writing competitions in a children's magazine. In addition, he was taking clarinet and piano lessons, he joined the church youth group, and he went to some Saturday morning art classes. We discovered a few other home educating families on the island and our families met monthly for mutual support, extra socialising opportunities, and a shared lunch.

Our younger son, however, preferred more structure to his days, and wanted to be able to track visible progress. He asked me regularly for a timetable, and for workbooks. He liked to discuss what he was doing, rather than learning on his own, and he wanted to be challenged. He was sometimes worried that he would not know enough to cope at secondary school.

Although his reading and writing were well ahead of typical age expectations, and his computer knowledge and competence a long way ahead of mine, he struggled with maths, and found it boring. Despite his insistence on a timetable, sometimes we barely managed half an hour of maths in a week. More often than not, it felt as if he were going nowhere, at least as far as maths was concerned.

2000-2002: commitment to home education

Our two years in Cyprus was clearly going to be extended considerably longer. But we had agreed that we would be in the UK at the end of 1999 to celebrate the turn of the century (and millennium). So we planned a couple of months' visit to the UK for December 1999 and January 2000, to see family and friends, and to have a break.

When we got in touch with the boys' old school in Birmingham, and asked if we could visit, our younger son was invited to join his former class, who were now Year Six, for as many days as he wished. He was delighted at the idea and kept telling us how much he had missed school. When he got there, he was thrilled to see his friends and to tell people about Cyprus. However, after the first few days he started complaining about the rigidity of school: of having to stop work at certain times, and of having to study particular topics rather than those which interested him.

What startled us more than anything was that, instead of having to work with the lowest maths group (as he had expected) he was put in the top group. He found even that work too easy. We had no idea how he could have become so proficient at maths. His classmates had been involved in the government's numeracy hour scheme, which meant that they had done at least forty minutes of maths every school day for the past two years — contrasted with our half an hour or less per week. They had done workbooks and tests and had covered many topics that we had barely touched upon. But our son, who was not mathematically inclined, had somehow managed to overtake them in conceptual understanding and ability.

This, we realised in retrospect, was a major turning point. It persuaded us all that home education is (or can be, depending on the child) a more efficient way of learning than a classroom. After three weeks at school, our son had no desire to return. Moreover, he decided that he did not want to go to secondary school in Cyprus after all. He was learning plenty of things at home, and he had a good social life. We had friends over regularly; he went to a Sunday School class he enjoyed. He had joined a choir, was doing well with piano lessons, and loved our home educators' get-togethers.

Back in Cyprus at the end of January 2000, we looked seriously, for the first time, at the likelihood that the boys would continue to be educated at home until they found jobs or went to university. But, we wondered, didn't everyone need A-levels, or at least GCSE exams, before they could do anything as adults...?

Further research led us to discover that although they could work towards GCSEs at home, it would be expensive and difficult to find someone to validate coursework abroad. It would be even more difficult (and expensive) to find somewhere to take the exams. An online friend mentioned an American Christian 'homeschool' course her children were following, which, she said, would give them certification equivalent to GCSEs and/or A-levels. We discussed it as a family, and looked at some sample workbooks which our friend sent us. We thought it looked interesting, if somewhat formal and US-centric. The main problem was the cost of the workbooks.

Then we found out, unexpectedly, that we were entitled to UK child benefit as we were still paying National Insurance and filing UK tax returns. Even better, we were sent a backdated amount to cover what we had missed since moving to Cyprus. This was quite a significant sum and would more than cover the initial registration, testing and the first few months' worth of workbooks of this curriculum. We took it as a sign to go ahead, so we registered.

It was encouraging to find that both boys tested at or ahead of their supposed grade level. The only initial problem with the certification programme was that it required that they begin at the 'eighth grade' level in a set number of subjects, even though in some they were both beyond that level. But we were able to work through the 'easy' ones quickly, and they helped us to become used to the style.

The idea was that students should set their own goals and work at their own speed. My job was to mark their work, and ensure that the final test for each workbook was done under supervision. We soon realised that it was a learning-by-rote system and that most questions were about comprehension or required short-term memory. While there were some parts that were interesting, and potentially useful, there was a lot that wasn't. Much of the work was tedious and there were days when nobody had any desire for doing anything.

In the meantime, both boys were continuing their piano lessons and the youth group. Our older son taught himself graphic art, skateboarding, and juggling. He played in the municipal marching band, took more art classes, and learned about sound mixing from his father. Our younger son sang in a Greek church choir and started guitar lessons. He learned about electronics, and how to wire plugs (again, not from me). Thankfully the academic curriculum work, when they did it, took no more than a couple of hours per day.

We had visitors, and saw historic sites, and talked about culture in Cyprus and worldwide. We played board games, read extensively, and continued to meet other home educators. There were some inevitable teenage problems: arguments, depression, a sense of futility, rampant hormones... I don't know if they were worse or better than they would have been if the boys had been in school. On the whole we stayed close as a family without, I hope, being over-protective.

2002-2005: looking at the future

A few months after he turned fifteen, our older son joined a local theatre group and was immediately involved in a fairly advanced teenage play. Within a few months he had played a major role in a production that won an international award, including a performance in London. The following year he took the Grade 8 drama exam with his class, and passed with honours. He took Grade 5 clarinet as well, although he had given up playing the piano.

He completed the first level of the American curriculum, and had the GCSE equivalent certificate. But by this stage he was pretty sure that he did not want to go to university. So he decided that he would not continue to the A-level equivalent courses. He thought he might like to be a graphic designer and website creator, and did some paid work designing sites for local hotels. However he quickly realised that he was not keen on working to a template as there was too little creativity involved. He took part in another theatre production, and wondered for a while if he might follow a career in drama. A year or two later, he considered studying musical instrument repair after an enjoyable and instructive afternoon in a repair shop learning to maintain his clarinet.

Our younger son, meanwhile, was playing the piano at quite a high level, including accompanying a band and choir at a concert, and regularly in church. He joined the youth band too. He was a long-term planner, and kept discussing possible careers. He thought about medicine at one point, but studying biology put him off. He thought about teaching, or going into the Anglican ministry, or writing, or doing electronics, or being a baker. He was always academically inclined, and thought that he would want to go to university, if possible.

I found this period one of the hardest, with the boys growing up and moving away from us emotionally. Sometimes they felt like misfits around their friends, although they had no desire to go to school. It worried me that I might be destroying their chances of a good future by educating them at home, even though it was a family decision and at every point appeared to be the best option available.

2005 and beyond

Shortly after he was eighteen, our older son volunteered for a couple of weeks on the Christian ship MV Doulos, best known for its large and inexpensive bookshop, which visited our town. He had a wonderful time and was excited about the potential of travelling around the world in a boat, talking to people about God, producing dramas, and providing books to churches and individuals. He decided to apply for a short-term programme on the ship, and was accepted for a three-month period when it was in Africa in the late summer of 2005.

It was difficult getting everything organised in time, including some essential vaccinations, but he got there, and he flourished. After he returned to Cyprus, enthused and inspired by his time on board, he decided he would apply to go back to the ship for two years, from January 2006.

Epilogue

So our older son finished the intermediate (A/S) level of the American curriculum course, deciding he might as well get the qualification even though he would probably never need it. I was devastated emotionally but at the same time excited for his future when he left home for two years, a few months after his nineteenth birthday.

He had no trouble fitting in with the multi-cultural environment on the ship. While there were inevitable stresses, he moved from being a 'deckie' to a 'waterman' within six months. When he did not know how to do something, he looked for someone to explain it to him. He took part in drama, puppet ministry, music, and country dancing. Then, with the knowledge he had gained from working alongside his father, he moved to the audio-visual team.

After a furlough he returned for a further two years, mostly working in the AV team, until the Doulos was de-commissioned at the end of 2009. He then worked for seven-and-a-half years in Carlisle. During this period he married a girl he met on the Doulos, and our first two grandchildren were born. In August 2017 our son and his family went for two years to the Logos Hope, sister ship to the Doulos.

Meanwhile our younger son also completed the intermediate stage of the curriculum programme we had been using, and decided he did not want to do another year of it. Instead, he started an Open degree course in theology, by correspondence, in the autumn of 2006. This was just before his eighteenth birthday. He very much enjoyed the academic study, although the online forums didn't have as much discussion as he had hoped. He struggled a little in his first essays, as he had never written anything academic before. However, he passed the first term, then agreed to let me proof-read (something the university recommended). As he developed a more academic style, and I helped him to edit run-on sentences and repetition, he started to achieve high marks.

It became evident that this would be a long road to a degree. So he decided to complete just the first level of the course. This took almost two years, but resulted in a certificate that was considered to be a higher standard than A-levels. During this time, he also volunteered for a couple of mornings each week in a local private primary school. It was now following a British curriculum and had a new and inspiring Head. Our son taught music and helped in classes, and thoroughly enjoyed the school environment as a young adult.

He decided to apply, through UCAS, for some teacher training courses in the UK. However, some of the staff at the school where he was volunteering recommended a normal degree followed by a PGCE (post-graduate certificate of education). So he also applied for some courses in theology. Newman, a small university in Birmingham, offered him a place on a degree course in theology for education.

The first year was easy for him, and he was able to fulfil a long-held desire to be the accompanying pianist for a young people's choir in Birmingham where he had sung many years previously. The pay was minimal but the experience was excellent, and enabled him to accept a better-paying job accompanying an adult choir that met just five minutes' walk from where he was living.

He graduated with a 2:1 that was only about half a mark away from a First, worked for a few months in a local IT company, and then did an MA in theology at Nottingham University. He accepted a teaching assistant post at the school where he had volunteered in Cyprus, and worked there for three years, including doing a PGCE in his final year.

In the spring of 2016, after three years in Cyprus, he applied for jobs in the UK and was offered one at a small private school in Surrey, teaching music. He started working there in September 2016 and is still happy there at the time of writing.

Finally

Every family is different. Each child has different dreams and abilities. Success can be measured in many ways. Degrees, well-paid jobs and happy family life are widely recognised 'successes', and many young people hope to achieve these things. But what matters most, in my view, is the sense of being in the right place, wherever that might be. That will most likely include challenges as well as outlets for creativity and a measure of contentment.

Home education taught my sons that they can take a step at a time: that they can put their minds to anything, if they believe it to be the right path.

References

Preface:

The home page of my original Geocities site in its first 'Wayback archive' snapshot, albeit with images, counters and links not working: https://web.archive.org/web/19991002062350/ http://www.geocities.com/heartland/lake/3262

The related Facebook page to the home-ed.info site: https://www.facebook.com/homeedinfouk/

Chapter One:

The 1996 Education Act: https://www.gov.uk/government/publications/elective-home-education

The Scottish Education Act: https://www.gov.scot/publications/home-education-guidance/

The default option for about a hundred and twenty years: https://en.wikipedia.org/wiki/Education_Act_1902

Formal education does not begin until a child is six or seven: see https://data.worldbank.org/indicator/SE.PRM.AGES (scroll down to 'all countries and economies')

Forms of differentiation: see, for instance, https://www.pearsonpublishing.co.uk/education/samples/S_494342.pdf

Chapter Two:

Negative kind of motivation: see https://www.alfiekohn.org/article/risks-rewards/

The drive to learn and achieve is innate: see https://www.psychologytoday.com/us/blog/freedom-learn/201712/the-joy-and-sorrow-rereading-holt-s-how-children-learn

Chapter Three:

More about de-registration and a sample letter: https://educationotherwise.org/index.php/deregistration

Chapter Four:

Online dictionary: https://www.dictionary.com/browse/education

Child's brain not the same as an adult one: see https://www.urmc.rochester.edu/encyclopedia/content.aspx?ContentTypeID=1&ContentID=3051

Benefits of reading aloud: see https://www.greatschools.org/gk/articles/read-aloud-to-children/

Screen time: see both https://www.psychologytoday.com/us/blog/behind-online-behavior/201604/what-screen-time-can-really-do-kids-brains and https://www.theguardian.com/media/2019/jan/04/screen-time-not-intrinsically-bad-for-children-say-doctors

Learning styles: see, for instance, https://www.mindtools.com/pages/article/vak-learning-styles.htm

Multiple Intelligences: see http://www.institute4learning.com/resources/articles/multiple-intelligences/

Mozart: see https://www.biography.com/people/wolfgang-mozart-9417115

Chapter Five:

Research shows: https://www.nheri.org/research-facts-on-homeschooling/

One dictionary reference: https://www.dictionary.com/browse/socialization

Helping shy children to socialise: see https://www.understood.org/en/friends-feelings/managing-feelings/loneliness-sadness-isolation/should-i-force-my-lonely-child-to-socialize-more

Chapter Six:

Parenting books referred to include:

Campbell, Ross, *How to Really Love your Child*

Leman, Kevin, *Making Children Mind Without Losing Yours*

Chapman, Gary, *The Five Love Languages of Children*

Faber, Adele and Mazlish, Elaine, *How to Talk so Kids will Listen and Listen so Kids will Talk*

Fortune-Wood, Jan, *Without Boundaries*

Prologue to part Two:

Literacy and Numeracy hours: see for instance http://news.bbc.co.uk/2/hi/uk_news/education/8120855.stm

Synthetic phonics: see https://www.theguardian.com/teacher-network/teacher-blog/2014/mar/04/reading-lessons-phonics-world-book-day

Chapter Seven:

Cuisenaire Rods: see https://sciencing.com/teach-math-cuisenaire-rods-7440838.html

Some online maths resources: http://home-ed.info/heresources/maths_resources

Chapter Eight:

Original National Curriculum English topics: see http://www.educationengland.org.uk/documents/pdfs/1999-nc-primary-handbook.pdf

Online English resources: see http://home-ed.info/heresources/english_resources

Print-on-demand: see, for instance, https://kdp.amazon.com/en_US/

Disadvantages of early reading: see https://www.independent.co.uk/news/education/schools/bethan-marshall-children-are-not-helped-by-reading-too-early-763182.html

Ages for learning new languages: see http://www.cal.org/earlylang/benefits/research_notes.html

Chapter Nine:

Recommended science books: see https://usborne.com/dynamic-content/subjects-honeypot-pages/science-books/ or the relevant publications at https://www.penguinrandomhouse.com/series/ACC/dk-eyewitness-books

General science resources online: http://home-ed.info/heresources/science_resources

Making a timeline: see, for instance, https://www.homeschooling-ideas.com/make-a-timeline.html

Range of topics for Religious Education: see https://assets.publishing.service.gov.uk/government/uploads/system/uploads/attachment_data/file/190260/DCSF-00114-2010.pdf

General RE resources online: http://home-ed.info/heresources/religious_resources

Art galleries online: see, for instance, https://www.nationalgallery.org.uk/paintings

Blender: https://www.blender.org/

Language resources online: see http://home-ed.info/heresources/language_resources

Chapter Ten:

UCAS site: https://www.ucas.com/

GCSE correspondence courses: http://home-ed.info/gcse_correspondence_courses

Open University: http://www.open.ac.uk/

Acknowledgements

It is customary to thank those involved in the production of a book. As explained in the introduction, this one has taken twenty years. Thus there are a lot of people who have, sometimes inadvertently, been inspirational or helpful.

Firstly, I want to thank the home educators whom I encountered on the UK home education forum twenty years ago. They were willing to answer almost endless questions, and managed to convince me that home education could be a positive option.

I am also grateful to the other former home educators who call themselves 'Fluff'; initially a light-hearted breakaway group from the more serious and focused home education forum, they have been a source of online support and friendship over many years. Several of them helped me to brainstorm ideas for a title for this book, something that was only determined about a week before publication.

In the off-line 'real' world, I am grateful to the Cyprus island-wide home educators with whom we met several times a year between 1998 and 2005. We played games, learned dances, went for walks and field trips. We camped together, and shared our lives and philosophies as well as acknowledging our problems. I learned a great deal from them all.

More recently I have been part of the Larnaka Christian writers' group. They have heard me read some of the material intended for this book, and offered useful critique. They have been an encouragement to me to keep writing over the past twelve years or so.

Since this book is self-published, the only person who was actively involved in its production is my husband. He took my text, formatted it suitably, and created the cover. The main inspiration, however, has been from our sons. They persuaded us to start home education, convinced us to continue, and turned out just fine despite my many mistakes. I am eternally grateful to them, to God, and to other family members and close friends who have supported and loved us in so many ways.